Advance Praise

"A must-read for any ambitious young woman (or man) who wants to get ahead. Sylvia Ann Hewlett provides actionable, hands-on advice—backed up with hard data and revealing stories from business leaders—for navigating the modern competitive workplace. Take her advice and run with it to the top."

—Anne Fulenwider, Editor in Chief, *Marie Claire*

"A mentor gives you advice about how to get ahead ⌐ r has power and uses it to get you a great assignmen⌐ ⌐mentored and undersponsored. Sylvi⌐ ⌐ need to know about how to make s ⌐mpany."

— ⌐essor of ⌐ Learning, Insead

"Sylvia Ann Hewlett is eno. ⌐usly insightful and always one step ahead. Reading this book makes it so obvious that having a sponsor—not a mentor—makes the critical difference, and I recommend it to both those aspiring to leadership roles and those looking to encourage the next generation of female talent."

—Helena Morrissey, CEO, Newton Investment
Management Limited; Chairman,
Opportunity Now; and founder, 30% Club

"This is a breakthrough book. Sylvia Ann Hewlett is challenging the entrenched orthodoxy that still prevents women and minority talent from scaling the heights. She argues convincingly that progress is more often a product of partnership than a solo success and tells us exactly how to make it happen. This study assembles hard evidence, compelling stories, and persuasive analysis and is invaluable to anyone who wants to get beyond 'do-gooding' to get the most out of their diverse talent."

—Trevor Phillips, former Chair, UK Equality and
Human Rights Commission

"For women climbing the ladder, Sylvia Hewlett has identified a key piece of the puzzle. High-potential women need sponsors who will not only provide advice but also actively create opportunities for their protégées to shine and advance. Hard work and merit are simply not enough to make it to the top."

—Anne-Marie Slaughter, author, "Why Women Still Can't Have It All"; Bert G. Kerstetter '66 University Professor of Politics and International Affairs, Princeton University; and former Director of Policy Planning, US Department of State

"This book takes executive development to a new place. By highlighting the key role sponsorship can play, Sylvia Ann Hewlett offers good career advice for individuals and provides a road map that companies can use to help ensure diversity at the top."

—Randall Stephenson, Chairman and CEO, AT&T

"We know the value of mentors to young professionals climbing the ladder, but Sylvia Ann Hewlett hits the mark in highlighting the tremendous power sponsors bring to that reach for the top. This is a significant work."

—James S. Turley, Chairman and CEO, Ernst & Young

"A powerful and urgent book. Sylvia Ann Hewlett demonstrates the heft of sponsors and shows how women and people of color can win sponsorship and take their place at decision-making tables. Heterogeneity at the top is not only fair, it unleashes creativity and the 'power of difference.'"

—Cornel West, Professor of Philosophy and Christian Practice, Union Theological Seminary

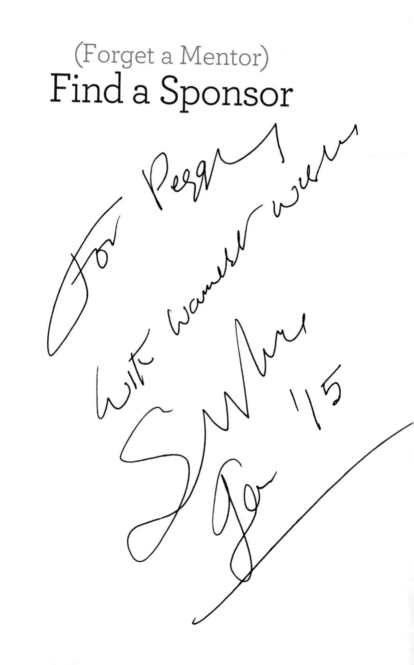

(Forget a Mentor)
Find a Sponsor

(Forget a Mentor)
Find a Sponsor

The New Way to Fast-Track Your Career

Sylvia Ann Hewlett

Harvard Business Review Press

Boston, Massachusetts

Printed in the United States of America

10 9 8 7

Library of Congress Cataloging-in-Publication Data

Hewlett, Sylvia Ann, 1946-

  Forget a mentor, find a sponsor : the new way to fast-track your career / Sylvia Ann Hewlett.
       pages. cm
  Includes bibliographical references.
  ISBN 978-1-4221-8716-6 (alk. paper)
  1. Career development. 2. Mentoring in business.
  3. Success in business. I. Title.
  HF5381.H4293 2013
  650.14--dc23

                              2013007357

The paper used in this publication meets the requirements of the American National Standard for Permanence of Paper for Publications and Documents in Libraries and Archives Z39.48-1992.

For my children
Shira, Lisa, David, Adam, and Emma,
may this book provide inspiration for your journeys

Contents

PART THREE

Pitfalls and Trip Wires

Acknowledgments

This book represents an unusual coming together of the personal and the professional, and it gives me particular pleasure to acknowledge the extensive help I've received from family and colleagues.

First and foremost I'd like to thank my husband Richard Weinert and our children, Shira, Lisa, David, Adam, and Emma. Their generous love has buoyed my spirits and lightened my load during the months I've spent wrapped up in this book. I am deeply appreciative of their support and understanding.

I owe a huge debt of gratitude to Melinda Marshall. Her deep knowledge of this subject matter and stellar writing skills contributed enormously to this book. I am extremely grateful to her.

My senior team Peggy Shiller, Lauren Leader-Chivée, Laura Sherbin, and Karen Sumberg have also been extraordinary. In particular, Peggy's management prowess and Laura's quantitative skills were critical in meeting the ambitious deadlines of this fast-track book. I thank them both.

I'm deeply grateful to the senior executives (and their companies) who underwrote and helped shape the survey research that underpins this book—Jennifer Christie, Kerrie Peraino, and Anré Williams (American Express), Debbie Storey (AT&T), Geri Thomas (Bank of America), Aimee George Leary (Booz Allen Hamilton), Erika D'Egidio (Bristol-Myers Squibb), Barbara Adachi (Deloitte), Dwight Robinson (Freddie Mac), Monica Poindexter (Genentech), Rosalind Hudnell (Intel), Fiona Cannon (Lloyds Banking Group), Keisha Smith and Jeffrey Siminoff (Morgan Stanley), Patricia Fili-Krushel, Patricia Langer, and Craig Robinson (NBCUniversal). Their generous support has gone well beyond funding. Over the past two years these corporate leaders provided precious access and lent wise counsel. A big thank you.

I am appreciative of the support of the co-chairs of the Task Force for Talent Innovation—Caroline Carr, Anthony Carter, Valerie Grillo, Deborah Elam, Anne Erni, Patricia Fili-Krushel, Gail Fierstein, Cassandra Frangos, Sandy Hoffman, Patricia Langer, Carolyn Buck Luce, Leena Nair, Lisa Garcia Quiroz, Craig Robinson, Lucy Sorrentini, Karyn Twaronite, and Melinda Wolfe—for their belief in the importance of this study, and their ongoing dedication to the mission of our organization.

A special word of thanks to Melinda Merino and Adi Ignatius of *Harvard Business Review*. Their commitment to this project was critical to getting this book off the ground. Thanks also to Courtney Cashman and Jennifer Waring at HBR for valuable contributions on the editorial front. I am hugely indebted to my daughter Lisa Weinert, the literary agent for this book, who encouraged me to transform dense research into much more narrative-driven prose. Her advice was spot on.

A word of thanks to Jennifer Abbondanza, Noni Allwood, Anita Bafna, Ella Bell, Wendy Berk, Cherie Booth Blair, Gail Blanke, Fleur Bothwick, Ken Bouver, Steve Burke, James Charrington, Kenneth Chenault, Sharda Cherwoo, Joanna Coles, Audrey Connolly, Jo Diamond, Danica Dilligard, Melinda Dodd, Brady Dougan, Ed Gadsden, Kent Gardiner, Eileen Garvey, Buck Gee, Joss Gill, Ed Gilligan, Kate Grussing, Sunita Holzer, Mellody Hobson, Linda Huber, Jane Hyun, Anne Jenkins, Charlotte Jones, Mike Kacsmar, Tasha Kersey, Laila Khan, Anand Kini, Sallie Krawcheck, Julita Lange, Paige Lillard, Janet Loesberg, Sian McIntyre, Tim Melville-Ross, Yvette Miley, Stacè Millender, Eleanor Mills, Helena Morrissey, Rajashree Nambiar, Iesha O'Deneal, Katherine Phillips, Trevor Phillips, Merima Platt, Adam Quinton, David Richardson, Steve Richardson, Rosa Ramos-Kwok, Farrell Redwine, Joy-Ann Reid, Dagmar Rosa-Bjorkeson, Jeanne Rosario, Amy Schulman, Todd Sears, Jane Shaw, Veronica Sheehan, Diana Solash, Xaio-Yu Song, Debora Spar, Ruth Spellman, Mark Stephanz, Joe Stringer, Peninah Thomson, Priya Trauber, Julie Watson,

Dan Wildman, Anne Williams, Donna Wilson, and Shawna Wilson—and all the women and men who took part in focus groups, interviews, and Insights In-Depth sessions.

I'm deeply appreciative of the research support and editorial talents of the CTI team: Michael Abrams, Joseph Cervone, Fabiola Dieudonné, Colin Elliott, Courtney Emerson, Christina Fargnoli, Catherine Fredman, Tara Gonsalves, Lawrence Jones, Anne Mathews, Andrea Turner Moffitt, Birgit Neu, Nicholas Sanders, Sandra Scharf, and Roopa Unnikrishan. I also want to thank Bill McCready, Stefan Subias, and the team at Knowledge Networks, who fielded the survey and were an invaluable resource throughout the course of this research.

Last but not least, a heartfelt thank you to the representatives of the seventy-five members of the Task Force for Talent Innovation for providing cutting-edge ideas and impressive amounts of collaborative energy: Elaine Aarons, Rohini Anand, Redia Anderson, Renee Anderson, Antoine Andrews, Diane Ashley, Nadine Augusta, Terri Austin, Ann Beynon, Anne Bodnar, Kenneth Charles, Daina Chiu, Tanya Clemons, Joel Cohen, Desiree Dancy, Nicola Davidson, Whitney Delich, Nancy Di Dia, Mike Dunford, Lance Emery, Linda Emery, Traci Entel, Nicole Erb, Anne Fulenwider, Michelle Gadsden-Williams, Trevor Gandy, Heide Gardner, Tim Goodell, Kathy Hannan, Kara Helander, Ginger Hildebrand, Alex Hiller, Ann Hollins, Kate Hoepfner-Karle, Celia Pohani Huber, Annalisa

Jenkins, Nia Joynson-Romanzina, Eman Khalifa, Inci Korkmaz, Denice Kronau, Janina Kugel, Frances Laserson, Janice Little, Yolanda Londono, Lori Massad, Donna-Marie Maxfield, Ana Duarte McCarthy, Beth McCormick, Mark McLane, Sylvester Mendoza, Carmen Middleton, Erica Nemser, Mark Palmer-Edgecumbe, Pamela Paul, Susan Reid, Kari Reston, Jennifer Rickard, Karin Risi, Jacqueline Rolf, Michael Springer, Eileen Taylor, Jennifer Tice, Lynn Utter, Cassy Van Dyke, Vera Vitels, Jo Weiss, Margaret Luciano-Williams, Meryl Zausner, and Fatemeh Ziai.

(Forget a Mentor)
Find a Sponsor

Introduction
My Story

My understanding of the power of sponsorship is rooted in my childhood. I grew up in a family of six sisters in a small town in the Welsh mining valleys. In the 1960s, this corner of Britain was a bleak and barren place. Across the coalfield, the collieries were closing down; unemployment hovered at 28 percent. As a girl child, there was not much you could look forward to. Maybe you could marry an unemployed miner? You could always do that.

But my father—very much the working-class bloke—had plans for his daughters. When I was thirteen, he took me by bus to Cambridge to show me the "dreaming spires" of one of Europe's most beautiful and distinguished universities.

After two days seeing the sights (Kings College Chapel and Trinity's Renaissance Library stand out in my memory) and taking in a debate at the Cambridge Union, my dad was ready to deliver *the message*. Over a plate of beans and toast (we'd found a cheap greasy spoon we felt comfortable in), he stared me in the eye and told me straight: "If you work hard, you can go here." His voice was hard-edged with urgent passion. "I promise you, girl, Cambridge will change your life." I was mesmerized.

My dad's advice was simple enough. But was it realistic? What chance did I have of getting in? I attended a third-rate state school that had never sent anyone to either Oxford or Cambridge. But it wasn't just my schooling, in a variety of ways I was a long way from being standard Oxbridge material. Until this bus trip, I had never eaten in a restaurant or stayed in a hotel, and I lacked some of the most elementary social skills. I had no small talk and was clueless when it came to figuring out which fork to use when tackling peas or fish. To cap things off, I spoke English with a thick Welsh accent—the kiss of death in upper-crust British society.

As it turned out, my father's challenge wasn't so unrealistic. My unsophisticated dad—quite unwittingly—had gotten it right. Times were a-changing and I did have a shot at getting into Oxbridge. A women's liberation movement was getting off the ground, and Harold Wilson (the new Labor prime minister) was kicking off a campaign to force the ancient universities to open their doors much more widely to two types of students: females and kids from the wrong side of the tracks. I qualified on both scores.

But I'm getting ahead of my story. After that trip to Cambridge, I returned to my mediocre Welsh school fired up and focused. I knew I had to ace both O- and A-levels and do very well on a barrage of highly specialized Oxford and Cambridge entrance examinations. The head teacher at my school washed her hands of the entrance exams, saying that the school could not offer preparation beyond A-level. But as I sent away for sets of past papers and delved in on my own, I got an offer of unofficial help from Miss Gwen Jones, my A-level English teacher. She told me I had special potential and that I reminded her of her sixteen-year-old self. Perhaps she wanted to provide the kind of support she herself had failed to find as a young person? Whatever the reason, Miss Jones offered invaluable help, assigning me challenging essays and giving me detailed feedback during the critical months leading up to A-levels and the Oxbridge entrance examinations. As Miss Jones saw it, she was not providing Oxbridge prep (by her own admission, she knew very little about the specifics of the examinations). Rather, she was trying to turn me into a good writer. She felt that if I learned to write with clarity and style, it might compensate for not being well drilled in other ways. We kept our tutoring sessions under the radar, meeting during lunch break and after classes in a small space under the stairs, away from the hustle and bustle of the school. We would cram two chairs under the stairwell and work away on essay drafts. I was enormously grateful for her practical help, but even more grateful for her belief in me. That someone in authority thought I had academic potential bolstered my resolve enormously.

Raw desire, a huge level of focus, and at least some hands-on help paid off. Four years later, I won admission to Cambridge University. I remember the scene so clearly: the telegram came on January 25—my birthday. My mum was feeling poorly (baby number six, born when she was forty-five-years old, had left her exhausted and depleted), and that Saturday morning she'd asked me to do a little clean up in our front garden (a rather grand word for the coal-dusted square of weeds that separated our semidetached house from the road). So I was tugging away at some soot-covered dandelions when the postman walked through the front gate holding a telltale manila envelope. My heart leaped into my mouth. I knew the drill because I had already been turned down by Oxford. Rejections came by regular post (why waste money on students you're turning down); acceptances came by telegram. Hands trembling, I grabbed the envelope, ripped it open, and read the magic words: "Offering place at Girton College, Cambridge University. Full scholarship. Letter following. Congratulations." I let out a piercing shriek, grabbed the amazed postman by the hand, and did a kind of furious stomping dance on the patch of dirt I'd just been digging.

Hearing the ruckus, three of my sisters ran out of the house. It took them a moment to figure out what was happening, but a grubby fist waving a manila telegram told the story and they joined in with gusto. I don't remember a happier day. I knew Cambridge would transform my life chances.

But how exactly did I get into one of the best universities in Europe? Even at the time, I realized that I didn't do this on my own. Sure, I took some of the credit (I had, after all, done an enormous amount of work), but I owed much to others. My dad was first on my list. Miss Gwen Jones was second. But I also was dimly aware of the contributions of Sally Alexander, a student activist who led the fight for equal access to education for British women, and Barbara Castle (a Minister in the Labor government who was spearheading new legislation on equal pay and equal opportunity). I didn't quite appreciate it at the time, but without these larger shifts in social attitudes and political priorities, I would not have gotten in. Oxbridge admissions committees were newly in the business of leaning over backward to see potential in candidates like me.

My years at Cambridge were almost as magical as my father promised. Despite some tough stuff on the social front (my accent and general lack of polish made it extremely difficult to fit into the upper-class student scene), by the middle of my first year I was under the wing of a remarkable woman who loved my spunk and determination and went to bat on my behalf. Dr. Jean Grove was a high-profile academic economist and my supervisor at Girton. Her support was transformative. A mere six months into my time at Cambridge, she chose me as her research assistant and invited me to accompany her on a summer research trip to Africa. She not only invited me to go, she made sure I could afford to take her up on the offer (my family was not in a position to bankroll a trip to Africa). That spring she sat down with me and painstakingly helped me apply for a foundation grant and then wrote the pivotal recommendation that ensured I got it.

Ghana was an extraordinary experience. We spent six weeks working with the Ewe tribe in the Volta Delta collecting agricultural data—crop yields, planting cycles, and so on. By the end of the summer, we'd accumulated enough evidence to demonstrate that the Ewe had developed a sustainable—and highly productive—type of intensive agriculture. They'd done this on their own using indigenous rather than imported methods and materials. It was a breakthrough finding.

My research assistantship in Ghana had huge payoffs for me. It fueled a lifelong interest in economic development and led to a coauthored article (with Jean Grove) that lifted my confidence and greatly improved my prospects for graduate school. Two years later, I won a spot at Harvard University—and a Kennedy Scholarship.

Post-Harvard and post–London University (where I earned my PhD), I landed a sought-after first job: as assistant professor of economics at Barnard College, Columbia

University, and began to forge what should have been a promising career in academe. I wish I could say that it was smooth sailing. It was not.

I made the classic female mistake. I thought that it was all about doing my job extraordinarily well. If I put my head down and worked as hard as I knew how, my value to the organization would be self-evident, and, of course, I would be recognized and promoted.

In retrospect, I could kick myself. Why didn't I understand that at these beginning stages of a serious and super competitive career, I needed a sponsor more than ever? Someone with power who believed in me and was prepared to propel and protect me as I set about climbing the ladder. Why didn't I get out there and look for a new Jean Grove?

Don't get me wrong; I did acquire a ton of supporters. Like many women, I was good at friendships, and during my time at Barnard, I developed mentoring relationships with several close female colleagues. One was an older woman—an historian named Annette Baxter—whom I admired for her kindness and her commitment to principle (she was forever on the outs with her chairman because she disagreed with the direction in which he was taking the department). Annette gave me a great deal. I remember with particular gratitude the ways in which she boosted my confidence and soothed my soul when I felt overwhelmed by the demands of a new baby, layered as it was on top of the pressures of a high-octane job. But close as our relationship was, Annette could not be my sponsor. She had little clout at Barnard (her feud with her department chair put her out of play), and her influence in my discipline (economics) was nonexistent.

My lack of sponsors had extremely serious consequences. Crunch time came seven years later, when I was up for tenure. In the months leading up to the decision, I was increasingly confident. I had always been an outstanding teacher—my ratings were off the charts—but I felt newly confident on the research front. My recent book had garnered stellar reviews and the attention of policy makers as well as scholars. As I helped my chairman assemble my dossier, I thought that it looked pretty impressive.

Imagine my shock when, three months later, I was denied tenure. My department supported me (I breezed by with a unanimous vote). The damage was done by the university-wide committee (the APT—Appointments, Promotion, and Tenure committee of Columbia University), which shot me down in a three-to-two vote. It turns out I had no advocates at this critical, final level. No one even knew me. According to a friend of a friend who knew something about the deliberations of the committee, the only thing about my seven-year track record that attracted the committee's attention was that I'd recently given birth to a premature baby. They feared this would "dilute my focus."

How did I deal with this massive setback? Not well. I had plowed twelve years of my life into this career of mine and I felt bewildered, betrayed, and brutally cast out. I mourned the waste of time and energy, but more importantly I mourned the loss of a beloved profession—one that I deeply valued and was exceptionally good at. Tenure decisions are "up" or "out"—you're either promoted to associate professor (and given lifetime job security) or you're fired. The decision came down in April, and by mid-May, I was packing up my office.

As I regrouped and attempted to figure out how to reinvent my professional life, one thing was sure: I'd learned my lesson on the sponsorship front. I now understood that climbing the ladder in any competitive field required heavy-duty support from a senior person with heft and influence.

Finding such a person wasn't easy. I hadn't been in the business of cultivating such relationships. But after some soul searching, I realized that I did have such a person in my back pocket. His name was Harvey Picker and he was dean of the School of International Affairs at Columbia University and former CEO of Picker Instruments. Picker wasn't particularly influential at Columbia (he didn't sit on any of the critical university-wide committees), but he did have power in the wider world, and most importantly, he was a great fan of mine. We'd met through my teaching. A Brazil enthusiast, Picker had sat in on some sessions of a course I taught on the Latin American economy, and we'd had spirited discussions on growth models and on trade-offs between economic growth and social justice in the Third World. We shared a Portuguese language instructor and a love of fado (Portuguese folk music).

A week after the tenure debacle, I turned up in Harvey's office clear-eyed and focused. I came directly to the point: could he help me find a job?

Harvey came through. Indeed, he was not merely responsive; he got out in front. In his old-fashioned courtly way, he told me that he'd learned of what he called "the ridiculous tenure decision" and was profoundly put out, so much so that he'd taken it upon himself to scope out a job that might suit me. The top slot at the Economic Policy Council (a New York–based nonprofit that brought together 100 corporate CEOs and trade union leaders to examine cutting-edge issues) was open, and Harvey thought that my skill set was perfect for the position. I had precisely the mix of top-notch academic credentials and international experience they were looking for. Did he have my permission to put my name forward? He knew the chairman of the EPC board rather well and while that didn't count for much (Harvey was a self-deprecating sort of person), it would open the door, which was all I needed. Dumbstruck, I conjured up a weak and wobbly yes. A month later, I started a brand-new career.

So I finally got it—sponsorship, that is. I did my utmost to never again let it go. My career journey was complicated (more on that in the final chapter). But from here on out, I knew that if I was going to amount to anything, I needed powerful sponsors.

PART ONE

The Sponsor Imperative

Who's pulling for you? Who's got your back? Who's putting your hat in the ring?

Odds are, this person is not a mentor but a sponsor.

Now don't get me wrong: mentors matter. You absolutely need them—they give valuable advice, build self-esteem, and provide an indispensable sounding board when you're unsure about next steps. But they are not your ticket to the top.

If you're interested in fast-tracking your career, in getting that next hot assignment or making more money, what you need is a sponsor. Sponsors give advice and guidance, but they also come through on much more important fronts. In particular they:

- Believe in your value and your potential and are prepared to link reputations and go out on a limb on your behalf.

- Have a voice at decision-making tables and are willing to be your champion—convincing others that you deserve a pay raise or a promotion.

- Are willing to give you air cover so that you can take risks. No one can accomplish great things in this world if they don't have a senior leader in their corner making it safe to fail.

It is this kind of heavy lifting that distinguishes a sponsor from a mentor. The data that underpins this book shows that sponsorship has a measurable impact on career progression. Men and women with sponsors are much more likely to rise up through the ranks and hang on to their ambition. Sponsors—unlike mentors—give you serious traction.

1

What Is Sponsorship?

Pat Fili-Krushel, chairman of NBCUniversal News Group, has come a long, long way in the super competitive and testosterone-fueled world of network news and media. Though not a journalist, she is the first woman in the American television news industry to head up a network news division, reporting directly to CEO Steve Burke. She's been on *Fortune* magazine's 50 Most Powerful Women list since 1998, and she's been honored with a slew of other awards, including induction into the Museum of Television & Radio's "She Made It" collection. No one would ever guess, in the presence of this poised and powerful executive, that she began her career as a secretary at ABC Sports.

"I've been lucky," Pat insists when I marvel at her extraordinary journey.[1] *"And* I've worked my tail off." She pauses to reflect, then adds, "But one of the things I've done well—and I don't know that it's conscious—is that I've always made my boss look good. All the people I've worked for will tell you, 'I like having Pat around, because I know she's got my back.'"

One of those people was Bob Iger, now CEO of Disney, whom she met at the Xerox machine when both were starting out their careers at ABC Sports. While she didn't initially report to Iger, her work ethic and performance won his attention and he pulled her onto his team. Whenever Iger moved up, he recommended that Fili-Krushel fill his vacancy. It was Iger who brought her over to ABC from Lifetime Television, where she'd served as a senior vice president of programming, and installed her as president of ABC Daytime television. But Fili-Krushel was quick to make good on his investment in her: she was the driving force behind "The View," the talk show that helped vault ABC's daytime programming to number one among women 18–49 years old. She also conceived and launched SoapNet, a 24-hour soap-opera cable network, which went on to become a multibillion-dollar business. "Do your job well, make sure your boss is fully informed, and don't be afraid to ask for help," she explains. "That's how you build the trust vital to any long-term professional relationship."

Superior performance and trust is certainly what delivered Pat to her current position with Steve Burke. She'd impressed him back when they both worked for Disney, she as president of ABC TV, he as president of ABC Broadcasting. "Pat was someone you could absolutely count on to do the right thing," Burke told me. "She wasn't intimidated by projects or people, and she didn't play politics. I knew her motivations at all times—and that made her one-hundred percent trustworthy."

So in 2011, after Comcast and GE merged with NBC and Burke found himself at the helm of a super-siloed media monolith, it was Pat he turned to for help in transforming the culture. "I knew if I got Pat, I wouldn't have to worry," he recalled. "I knew when she found things wrong, she would make them right. I knew that if any of our top people had exposure to her, even without exposure to me, they'd know the kind of company we were trying to create."

Hired on as executive vice president of NBCUniversal, Pat immediately set to rights the compensation structure that had mired Burke's team in the past. With her formidable people skills, she helped effect the collaborative culture that Burke had envisioned. When Burke decided to form the News Group, putting NBC News, CNBC, MSNBC, and The Weather Channel in the hands of one executive, it was again Pat who emerged as first choice. "I knew my decision would ruffle some feathers," Burke confided. "Pat's not a journalist, so how could she be put in charge of hundreds of journalists who are risking their lives all over the world? But she didn't need to be the senior-most journalist in order to find the people who could make this new environment productive and cooperative."

But if initially people scratched their heads at Pat's appointment, they don't anymore. "Everyone, from Brian Williams to staff members, has told me she's a breath of fresh air," Burke observed when we spoke in early 2013. "Pat's a great executive, the kind who creates an environment where people enjoy what they do. She has my complete confidence."

Marina, an assistant finance manager at Lloyds Banking Group of London, feels pretty well supported at work.[2] She received a warm welcome when she returned from maternity leave last year. She was given the part-time schedule she'd requested—an unusual accommodation for anyone in the risk assurance department—and was assigned to a line manager she both liked and knew would look out for her.

While grateful for these developments, Marina wasn't terribly surprised. She believed that it was all about performance, and she'd consistently delivered over her ten years at the bank. "It stands to reason," she told me, "that the higher-ups appreciate my track record. When you have worked for a company as long as I have, your results speak for themselves," she explained. "Once someone has seen your good work it's hard for someone to say, 'Oh she's rubbish, she's got to go,' because people won't believe it. People who know my skills and level of commitment will support me and make sure I'm rewarded."

But it doesn't seem to be working out that way. Now that she's working a full-time schedule again, Marina is frustrated that those same people haven't done more to fast-track her career. One of them, "a super-duper female executive" she met through the women's network at the bank, struck her as someone who might be a champion. "She's absolutely my role model because she also has young children and knows a thing or two about how a woman can make it big in a male-dominated environment," Marina enthused. But their relationship has remained casual—and remote. "I thought of asking her to sponsor me," said Marina wistfully, "but I had second thoughts. She's my boss's boss and there might be some conflict of interest."

For now Marina is pinning her hopes on her long-time mentor—a senior person who has given her wise counsel over the years. He makes a point of complimenting her on her contributions, so she's fairly sure that he has sent some work her way. "No one has said that directly, but I have a feeling that's the case," Marina said. "He did say to me once, 'You're one of those people who's good at fixing things. You're Mrs. Fixit.'"

Marina told me that she thinks in time her mentor will come through. Having recognized her good work, he will eventually reward it. "I'm definitely on his radar" she says, citing a conversation where he seemed pleased to learn she was working on a mission-critical project. "I haven't gotten a promotion out of him yet, but I'm confident he sees my potential."

Two ambitious women, two different career strategies. Top performers with a great deal of potential, each attracted the attention of a superior positioned to help her navigate a particularly tricky curve in her career trajectory. But whereas Marina is still waiting for her promotion, Pat has ascended to the "C-suite" (the domain of CEOs, CFOs, COOs, and other chief executives).

What accounts for these vastly different outcomes? Why do so many women, like Marina, stall out short of the leadership positions they have the potential to fill? Why do so few women, like Pat, fulfill their dreams and attain positions of true power and influence?

After two years of exhaustive inquiry, I can tell you why: high-potential women have mentors but lack sponsors. They fail to cultivate strategic alliances with individuals capable of propelling them into leadership positions and protecting them from other contenders. Often, like Marina, they have would-be advocates, senior-level leaders who've taken note of their capabilities. But they don't know how to turbocharge these relationships. They don't understand the quid pro quo, the mutual investment that ensures both parties remain incentivized to help each other over the long run. So, like Marina, they put their heads down, work harder, and wait, hoping that their mentors and role models will see to their success.

This mistake is all too common and one that women and professionals of color are particularly prone to making. I myself have made it. But as my own career path demonstrates, it's never too late to seize hold of your dreams, win sponsors, and pull yourself out of a career stall. If you're on a slow road to nowhere, consider changing your strategy. Forget a mentor. Find a sponsor.

Mentorship versus Sponsorship

Don't get me wrong: mentors matter. You absolutely need them. But they're not your ticket to the top. Mentors give, whereas sponsors *invest*.

Let me clarify.

Mentors are those people who take an interest in counseling you because they like you, or because you remind them of themselves. Mentors will listen sympathetically to just about anything you care to bring up. Indeed, the whole idea of having a mentor is to discuss what you cannot or dare not bring up with your boss or colleagues. Your mentor will listen to your issues, offer advice, and review which problem-solving approaches to take and which to discard. Mentors give generously of their time. In return, you listen and try to heed their advice. It may be that they enjoy drawing on their experience and sharing their wisdom, or they're paying back their own early supporters, or they're paying the debt forward. In any case, it's an asymmetric relationship. The energy is flowing one way: toward you.

A *sponsor*, as we shall explore, is also someone who takes an interest in you and your career, but not out of altruism or like-mindedness. A sponsor sees furthering your career as an important investment in his or her *own* career, organization, or vision. Sponsors may advise or steer you, but their chief role is to develop you as a leader. Your role is to earn their investment in you. Indeed, throughout the relationship, you're delivering outstanding results, building their brand or legacy, and generally making them look good. You're driving the relationship, making sure that whatever dividends you realize in the way of promotions, pay raises, or plum assignments are manifestly dividends that you earned. Sponsorship, done right, is transactional. It's an implicit or even explicit strategic alliance, a long-range quid pro quo. But provided you're giving as good as you're getting, there's nothing about this dynamic that warrants distaste. Sponsorship isn't favoritism or politics; it doesn't rig the game. On the contrary, it ensures you get what you've worked for and deserve. (See figure 1-1 for a comparison of the two roles.)

FIGURE 1-1

Sponsor versus mentor

		Mentor
Sponsor	**Sponsor/ Mentor**	• Experienced person willing to help and support you
• Senior person who believes in your potential and is willing to take a bet on you	• Advice	• Builds your confidence and provides a sounding board
• Advocates for your next promotion	• Guidance	• Offers empathy and a shoulder to cry on
• Encourages you to take risks and has your back	• Makes introductions	• Expects very little in return
• Expects a great deal from you (stellar performance and loyalty)	• Gives feedback	

Sponsors can be *role models*, leaders you relate to and aspire to emulate. But they needn't be, and often aren't. What's important in sponsorship is trust, not affinity. It'd be nice if the person who can most help you turns out to be a person you like or most want to *be* like. But trust can arise between two people who are vastly different. This difference imbues sponsorship with power, because each party gains from the complementarity of the other. The alliance is then greater than the sum of its individual parts.

This is not to belittle the role that *supporters*, by which I mean both mentors and role models, play in your career. Role models serve as vital inspiration, boosting your drive and giving form to your ambition. Mentors, who are often role models, can offer empathetic support, help you figure out what you want, and determine with you what steps will get you there. A good mentor will decode the unwritten rules, demystify the way things work, and offer you tips on navigating the organization. People who are mentored feel less isolated (especially if they're entrepreneurs), more connected to their company, and less stressed than those who lack such attention and guidance. Multicultural professionals in particular benefit from the emotional support and pledge of solidarity that mentors and role models of color provide.

But neither mentors nor role models can give you real career traction. Research we conducted at the Center for Talent Innovation (CTI) shows that sponsors, not mentors, put you on the path to power and influence by affecting three things: pay raises, high-profile assignments, and promotions. When it comes to asking for a pay raise, our research finds, the majority of men (67 percent) and women (70 percent) resist confronting their boss.[3] With a sponsor in their corner, however, nearly half of men and 38 percent of women will make the request—and, our focus-group research suggests, will succeed in getting the raise. When it comes to getting assigned to a high-visibility team or plum project, some 43 percent of male employees and 36 percent of females will approach their manager and make the request. With a sponsor, the numbers rise to 56 percent and 44 percent, respectively.

Our research also shows that the individuals who are most satisfied with their rate of advancement are individuals with sponsors. Fully 70 percent of sponsored men and 68 percent of sponsored women feel they are progressing through the ranks at a satisfactory pace, compared to 57 percent of their unsponsored peers. That translates into a "sponsor effect" of 23 percent for men and 19 percent for women. CTI research shows that sponsors affect women's career trajectory even more profoundly than men's in at least one respect: 85 percent of mothers (employed full-time) who have sponsors stay in the game, compared to only 58 percent of those going it alone. That's a sponsor effect of 27 percent.

The sponsor effect on professionals of color is even more impressive. Minority employees are 65 percent more likely than their unsponsored cohorts to be satisfied with their rate of advancement.

Even in companies with robust mentoring programs, mentoring doesn't deliver on its promise, or at least not for women and people of color. Research conducted by Catalyst (an advocacy organization for women in business) shows that while more women than men have been mentored, more men have won promotions—15 percent more, according to a 2008 study.[4] Mentors are no silver bullet, no matter how heavily *Fortune* 500 corporations invest in mentorship programs. So if, like Marina, you're waiting for your role model or mentor to part the waters and set you up on the distant shore, you're wasting precious time.

I wrote this book to make sure you don't make Marina's mistake: to show you why you need sponsors (and you need more than one) to help you achieve your vision, whether that's a leading role in a large company, a strategic role in a small company, founding a business of your own, or steering a nonprofit or educational organization to fulfill its mission and mandate. I created the road map you'll find in part II to show you exactly what you need to do to attract sponsors, win their advocacy, sustain their interest, and leverage their backing throughout your career. Because even at the pinnacle of your career, you'll find that these skills serve you. Fabulously successful entrepreneurs and CEOs alike still need powerful voices to get them onto boards, introduce them to investors, or secure them a spot at the World Economic Forum at Davos. Sponsorship is the mechanism by which people of vision attain their goals, which is why no one—male or female, millennial or boomer, start-up employee or multinational manager—can afford to dismiss it or miss out on it.

That being said, women and people of color stand to benefit the most from this book precisely because sponsorship has long been the inside track for Caucasian men. Men are 46 percent more likely than women, and Caucasians are 63 percent more likely than professionals of color, to have a sponsor seeing to their success. I'm not suggesting there's a conspiracy here. Rather, it's a quirk of human nature that keeps leadership in the United States and Europe mostly pale and male. Those in power tend to invest in other members of their tribe because they're the ones they trust most readily. This is the way it has worked since the dawn of civilization.

But that doesn't mean sponsorship is the exclusive province of straight white guys. That sponsorship has worked so well for the old boys' network for so long simply underscores the power of this type of advocacy, not the exclusivity of power.

As the founder of an organization focused on talent issues, I have the privilege of knowing white male executives who are committing every resource at their disposal to changing the face of leadership, and not because women's groups have pressured them into it. They understand that much of the best talent out there is diverse. Our research shows that Caucasian men comprise a mere 17 percent of college graduates around the world.[5] There's never been a better time, that is, for accomplished, ambitious women and people of color to show they're eager to move into leadership roles, because the business sector is competing for them worldwide. For them, sponsorship is the key that turns all the tumblers, unlocking the door to the C-suite, on Main Street as well as Wall Street.

The research undergirding the advice in this book draws on the collective experience and wisdom of some ten thousand full-time workers in the private sector.[6] We interviewed dozens of *Fortune* 500 leaders, convened with over a hundred managers in on-site and online focus groups, and surveyed thousands of employees in the United States and the United Kingdom—people on every rung of the ladder in every profession that requires a college degree. While most of these people work for large corporations, the insights derived from their experience transcend environment. Cultivating a sponsor and leveraging the relationship to mutual benefit turns out to be a skill that serves people in nonprofits and education as readily as it serves people in for-profits and government.

Finally, I've tested this research on the ground. I've presented this road map to hundreds of professionals worldwide, to graduate students at Skolkovo School of Management in Moscow, to bankers in London's City, even to the National Football League in midtown Manhattan. The response has been amazing. You can feel the "aha!" moment happen. Men and women see, in sponsorship, the game changer they've been looking for. But they see something more: with this road map in hand, they're in a position to do the changing. They don't need to wait. They don't need to be tapped or chosen or singled out by someone else. It's up to them to put this dynamic into play.

And now, it's up to you.

2

How Sponsorship Works

In 1983, barely two years out of business school, Brady Dougan accepted what many would have considered a mission impossible: relocating to Japan to take over the derivatives business in the regional office, grow its staff, and set a strategic course to build the firm's Pacific Rim presence in that business. Having only joined the derivatives group of Bankers Trust in 1982, Dougan had little business experience and no background in the region. Nor did he speak Japanese. He was all of twenty-four years old.

Today, Dougan is CEO of the financial powerhouse, Credit Suisse. He looks back on his first breakthrough assignment with wonder, marveling at the extraordinary opportunity he was given and amazed that his boss placed such trust and faith in him to deliver. "I did have a strong feel for my role and my duties," he says, "and I enjoyed the challenge of doing new things. But to ask me to take charge in Japan and grow the derivatives business for the entire Pacific Rim on my own? I was a very young manager to be doing that."

Dougan credits his ascent to his boss, to whom he reported for nearly twenty years, not because he made it easy for Dougan, but because he made it hard. "I became the person he gave the toughest assignments to, the things that needed fixing," Dougan observes. "He piled on the responsibilities. But because he believed in me—because he was clearly betting on me and giving me a leg up—I felt I owed him a lot and should do whatever he asked and come through with whatever he needed. That Japan posting proved to be an incredible opportunity. This sponsor of mine not only believed I was going to be successful, he then did everything he could to help me succeed." For example, Dougan's boss lent unvarnished feedback and wise counsel as needed and helped Dougan figure out how to meet targets and fit his operation into the larger context of the business. When Dougan stumbled, his boss came to his defense. "He'd say to senior management, 'Okay, this didn't go perfectly, but Brady's overall record is very strong,'" Dougan explains. "He was always ready to run interference, manage the internal politics for me. That gave me the breathing room to take risks. And in this industry, you have to take a risk. Because only by doing so do others learn to believe in your ultimate potential."

What a Sponsor Does

Dougan's extraordinary career ascent attests to the power of sponsorship. Indeed, he is so sure of its value that he spearheaded a successful initiative at Credit Suisse that turbocharges the careers of high-potential women. As Dougan knows full well, sponsorship can help catapult a top performer into senior management, as well as expand the reach and impact of senior leadership. It's the secret sauce, the missing link, the invisible dynamic that accounts for who is, and who isn't, in power, whether that person is steering a *Fortune* 500 company or an Internet start-up, whether that person founds a nonprofit or chairs an academic committee. Everyone who has realized an amazing vision or exerts remarkable influence can and will point to a series of sponsors, powerful individuals who helped pull them up or fund their ventures or clear a path forward. There are no exceptions.

Sponsors do three things that mentors do not. Dougan's sponsor, for instance, went out on a limb for his protégé, installing him at the helm of his pet project. Having plunged his protégé into uncharted waters, he provided just enough support to keep Dougan afloat, both in Japan and within the firm, talking up his talent whenever others were eager to disparage it. Most importantly, he provided him air cover, acting as a shield so that Dougan could take the risks the assignment demanded. Having chosen to invest in this particular young man, this sponsor understood he needed to do everything within his power to ensure that Dougan, and the Pacific Rim project, proved to be a resounding success.

CTI research, begun in 2010, affirms the centrality of these three functions. In addition, we also learned that a sponsor does at least two of the following: he or she will expand your perception of what you can do; connect you to other senior leaders; boost your visibility in the company; provide you with stretch opportunities; advise you on your presentation of self; connect you to clients or customers; and give you honest, critical feedback on where you need to improve your game. (See table 2-1 for a summary of a sponsor's roles and responsibilities.)

TABLE 2-1

What is a sponsor?

Delivers high-octane advocacy

A sponsor is a senior leader who, at a minimum:	And comes through on at least two of the following fronts:
• Believes in me and goes out on a limb on my behalf	• Expands my perception of what I can do
• Advocates for my next promotion	• Makes connections to senior leaders
• Provides "air cover" so I can take risks	• Promotes my visibility
	• Provides stretch opportunities
	• Gives advice on "presentation of self"
	• Makes connections to clients/ customers
	• Gives honest/critical feedback on skill gaps

If you're not in a corporate setting, it may help to think of a sponsor as a talent scout. He'll get you in front of directors to audition for a key role. He'll also nudge the director to choose you. But his investment in you doesn't stop there. He'll coach you on your performance so that you prove to others what an excellent choice he made. He'll focus a spotlight on you so that other directors take note of your abilities, and he'll make introductions afterward so that you can follow up with them to bring your talent to a wider audience. Should you stumble, or should any of those other directors turn hostile, your sponsor will come to your aid, because now that your brands are linked, it's in his best interests to ensure you succeed.

Of course, sponsors also provide advice, which is why they're confused with mentors. From CTI's survey research it's clear that protégés expect advice from their sponsors. Fully 74 percent of respondents told us they looked to a sponsor to provide unvarnished feedback. But it's important to distinguish the critical feedback that sponsors deliver from the kindly advice mentors might dispense when asked. When a sponsor discusses your strengths and weaknesses, it's with an eye to steering you along a certain trajectory, one that will provide strategic gain for both of you. To that end, sponsors will not hesitate to point out painful shortcomings— skill gaps, communication failures, appearance blunders. They'll also tell you where and how to acquire critical line experience, build key networks, and project executive presence, which comprises looking and acting the part of a leader in terms of appearance, presentation skills, and gravitas (more on this in chapter 12). This kind of strategic feedback can be awfully hard to hear. Yet because of sponsors who articulate the unspoken and point out the unremarked, women and people of color get to crack the code of an organization, overcoming hidden biases to lever themselves into contention for the top slots.

One African American banking executive told me how he's come to feel a "blood tie" with his sponsor, precisely because she's asked him to take some difficult, even painful steps to improve himself. "A sponsor will smack you harder to shape up," he observed, "but will protect you as you move to the next level. She'll tell you the sort of things you'd never know were said about you in a meeting and would otherwise never know to correct. And if she's really got your back, she'll tell you how to correct them."

A sponsor's protection goes beyond delivering tough love, our interviewees affirmed. One tax attorney described how he supported his protégé all the way to partnership, having hired her in the first place. He was confident of her ability to deliver and when long-term clients demurred at liaising primarily with a junior person, this attorney vouched for her expertise. When she became the target of unfair criticism by another partner, he intervened, extorting from that partner an apology and a promise to look at the evidence and be less judgmental. In subtle and overt ways, he ensured that she was able to thrive, which indeed she did, making partner in four years.

Unlike mentors, that is, sponsors will go the extra mile, taking you aside to tell you what you absolutely need to know, taking detractors aside so they don't impede your progress, and clearing a path forward should you encounter obstacles. Sponsors make it their business to see you succeed because you carry their brand. You're an extension of them, a carrier of their torch, the putative implementer of their vision. It behooves them to do everything in their power, once they believe in you and they've chosen you, to keep you on track. Only by seeing you to the finish line can they protect their own reputation.

Kerrie Peraino, now a senior vice president at American Express heading up international human resources and global employee relations, describes how her supervisor kept her on track for management at a juncture in her career when other women in her position might have been derailed for good. Some years earlier, just after she'd given birth to her second child, Peraino asked for a three-day-a-week schedule. She was a mid-level manager and felt confident she could perform her duties in a compressed workweek, but also recognized her superiors might not see it that way. "That's when my sponsor went to bat for me," Peraino relates. "She knew I was fully committed, not just to my team but to the firm, and she was determined to give me whatever support or air cover I needed to keep me on track." Peraino's request was granted and, after three years of working part-time, she was made a vice president—a testament not only to her hard work, but also to her sponsor's committed support and advocacy. "I look back on that phase and think how my career might have played out differently were it not for her sponsorship," Peraino muses. "I really don't think I'd be where I am today. I might even have left the firm. Since she placed such trust in me and went out on a limb to offer a flexible work arrangement, I was determined to be a credit to her."

During economic downturns or industry upheavals, a sponsor can be the voice in the room that ensures you keep your job. One executive I interviewed recalled a watershed moment when her sponsor flew in to London from New York to secure her a promotion she was in danger of losing to an outsider. "Marcia marched into the chairman's office, put her badge on the table, and said that it was completely transparent what was happening and that if I didn't get the job, we were both leaving," she related. "Her strong-arm tactics worked, because she was tremendously valued. They decided to go ahead and appoint me."

When your job is on the line, your sponsor can at least ensure you don't damage your career over the long term. Darren, a director in the advisory practice of a large accounting firm, told me how he went to bat for a protégé about to be fired because he'd been part of a group that had engaged in less-than-ethical practices in the run-up to the global financial crisis. "I did not just buckle over and go with the groupthink about the treatment this guy should get," Darren recalls. "I felt he was being unfairly tarnished, and I let my feelings be known to my peers as well as the people he reported to." When that didn't work—he was outnumbered and outvoted—he counseled his protégé to "take control of his destiny" and quit, so that he could leverage his track record without the stain of a job termination. Darren made introductions and spoke favorably on his protégé's behalf, an effort that culminated in a job offer at another "Big Four" accounting firm where the executive could distance himself from the events of 2008. "I may not have saved his job, but I believe I did save his career," says Darren.

What a Protégé Does

Maria, a managing director at a financial services firm with nine hundred technology professionals reporting to her, has always been a hard worker and a strong performer. Even employees whose jobs she's eliminated speak highly of her. She's come a long way from Dominica, where she was born, and Washington Heights, where she grew up. Still, as a dark-complexioned Latina leading overwhelmingly white male teams, she recognizes that being a subject-matter expert and a star producer don't, in and of themselves, account for her leadership position. "I've always had the backing of my superiors," she says, "because I've always made sure they succeeded at whatever they were doing."

Her first sponsor was a colleague who became her boss. He'd signed up to lead an integration project—for the chief investment officer, and she signed up to help him. It proved to be a highly stressful, cross-functional project that eliminated a number of jobs and tested the skills of her sponsor as well as her own. Maria didn't let him down, bringing the project to a successful close in ten months. But what endeared her to the CIO, in addition to her remarkable client-service skills, was her unflagging commitment to him. "I was his right-hand person," she says. "I made sure that he was not surprised by anything. The thing about tech, systems are always breaking down and I was there for him. When things were going poorly I was the person saying, 'Have you thought about this?'"

At one point, the company experienced a major data-center failure the day before Maria was to fly to California to receive a prestigious award from a Hispanic science and technology group. "It was a great honor. I was all packed and ready to go," she recalls. But an hour before departure, she got a call from her sponsor. There was a crisis at work. So she canceled her plans and stayed to help. Afterward he told her, "I will always remember this. Thank you for always being there for me."

And remember he did. When Maria was struggling to pull out of a career stall, he worked with her to devise a way forward, ultimately helping her land a coveted managing director position. His intervention marked a real turning point. "If you have a history of delivering, being there, being committed, and making sure your boss is successful, he or she will be there to pick you up," says Maria. "No one's going to do that for someone who has let them down."

What protégés do, in a word, is *deliver*. As Maria intuited early in her career, they come through with both stellar performance and die-hard loyalty. They also deliver a distinct personal brand or unique skill set, a critical finding of the research. Star performers are very likely to attract sponsors, and loyal performers are very likely to keep them. But if they fail to distinguish themselves, these loyal performers run the risk of becoming permanent seconds, lieutenants who never make captain. To position themselves for the top job, protégés must therefore contribute something the leader prizes but may intrinsically lack: gender smarts or cultural fluency on a team that lacks diversity; quantitative skills or technical savvy on a team that is deficient in hard expertise; people skills on a team that's bristling with eggheads and nerds. You could provide unique insight into a target market. You could have access to a sought-after circle of investors or stakeholders. Whatever you bring, it must burnish the sponsor's personal brand across the organization even as it distinguishes you from the crowd, delivering you your dream job and not one as second-in-command.

Maria, for example, distinguished herself on the integration project by using her built-in proclivity (born of her culture and her heritage) to treat everyone on the team as if they were family. "I'm Latin and I'm very family-oriented," she explains. "When I'm in charge, I want to know, 'How's your baby doing? Are you getting enough sleep?' That's one of the things people love about being in my group. I make sure it's warm, supportive, and open." It's one of the things about her that secured the support of her first sponsor ("He told me never to change, no matter how rigid the manager I reported to") and intrigues her current sponsor. "You're very effective," he told her. "You have some people skills that I need to lean on and learn from."

This isn't to diminish the performance piece of this equation. Delivering a superior product on time, winning a key piece of business, innovating a solution, and otherwise driving results with bottom-line impact are what will attract the attention of a sponsor in the first place. A third of US managers and nearly half of UK managers want to sponsor a "producer," a go-getter who hits deadlines. "I don't think for a second that my sponsor would promote me if I didn't deliver superior results," the head of audit at Lloyds observes. "I don't feel that I can rest on my laurels just because I have her sponsorship." A partner in Ernst & Young's London advisory group stressed, in an interview, his key considerations when deciding whom to back: "It's simple," he said. "Hard work and drive. Are they the kind of person who has a work ethic similar to mine?" he asks himself and, "Will they go the extra mile?"

Debbie Storey, chief of diversity at AT&T, agrees. "It's all about understanding the company's goals and direction, then making things happen. It's about continuously innovating and leading change," she says. "They have to demonstrate by *how* they lead that they can consistently drive teams to achieve results."

While performance and value added will make you indispensable to your sponsors, it is loyalty that will bind them to you and make them care about your success. Thirty-seven percent of male managers (and 36 percent of female managers) say that being a loyal protégé matters, more than being collaborative or visionary or even highly productive. If delivering a standout performance is what *wins* you the attention of the powerful, demonstrating loyalty is what guarantees a powerful leader will commit to sponsoring you over the long haul. (See table 2-2 for our definition of a protégé.)

TABLE 2-2

What is a protégé?

Delivers high-octane support

A protégé is a high-potential employee who, at a minimum:	And comes through on at least two of the following fronts:
• Outperforms—contributes 110%	• Is trustworthy and discreet
• Is loyal to me and the organization	• Covers my back
• Contributes a distinct personal brand	• Promotes my legacy
	• Brings "value added"—different perspective/skill sets
	• Leads with a "yes"
	• "Burnishes my brand" across the organization
	• Builds my "A" team

As many of the executives in our survey pointed out, loyalty means looking out for your sponsor as protectively as your sponsor looks out for you. "Protégés can provide insights about what's happening lower down in the organization, because when you're at a senior level, you're less likely to get those honest messages about what people think of you and your strategy," says Lloyds' head of audit, who acts as her sponsor's eyes and ears and exhorts her protégés to do the same for her. Ed Gadsden, former chief diversity officer at Pfizer, remembers asking his sponsor, the legal scholar and federal judge Leon Higginbotham, why he took such an interest in him, aside from the fact that they were both African American. "You're nothing like me, Ed," Higginbotham told him. "The people you're around, the things you see, what you're hearing—you provide a perspective I wouldn't otherwise have." Now, as a sponsor himself, Gadsden has come to appreciate the perspective his own protégés provide: "They make sure I'm never blindsided," he says.[1]

Just as your sponsor is someone who supports you when you're not in the room, so too must you protect him or her from employee gossip, from harsh outsider opinion, even from collegial criticism. "Who do you want in your bunker?" an African American executive at Johnson & Johnson asked me in an interview, "A loyal comrade-in-arms who, if you turn your back, guns for you, not at you."

The Two-Way Street

What should be clear, at this point, is how extraordinarily *reciprocal* sponsorship is. Protégés attract sponsors by delivering in exceptional ways and secure sponsorship by remaining utterly devoted, even as they distinguish themselves as stars in their own right. In return, sponsors invest in their protégés, not because they're impelled to pay it forward but because they recognize the incredible benefit to their own careers of building a loyal cadre of outstanding performers who can extend their reach, build their legacy, and burnish their reputation. Over time, both parties win. Indeed, the win-win aspect of sponsorship is what accounts for its extraordinary leverage and durability. (See figure 2-1.)

FIGURE 2-1

The two-way street

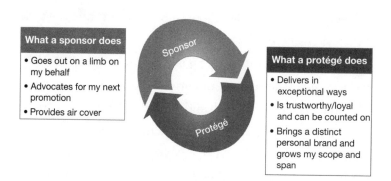

What a sponsor does
- Goes out on a limb on my behalf
- Advocates for my next promotion
- Provides air cover

What a protégé does
- Delivers in exceptional ways
- Is trustworthy/loyal and can be counted on
- Brings a distinct personal brand and grows my scope and span

Contrast this to the decidedly one-way street of mentorship. Mentors give: they devote time, impart wisdom, and act as a sounding board (or a shoulder to cry on). But mentees merely recieve: they have no particular responsibilities other than to show up and listen. Mentors take an interest in the mentee's career, but not a stake in it, as they're not going to be held accountable for outcomes. Mentorship is at heart an expenditure rather than an investment, a gift rather than an alliance. It's doomed to peter out: the mentee outgrows the mentor's range of experience, the mentor moves on to needier novitiates.

What this means is that the nature of your support relationships is *up to you.* You'll get back what you put in. If you're a high-potential or strong performer, you'll attract the interest of your superiors, but whether that interest translates into mentorship or sponsorship is a function of your investment. You might be tapped for development, but you're not going to be given a ride on the coattails of anyone who doesn't see you pulling your weight (and then some). Mentors may pick you, but *you* pick your sponsors by committing yourself to their best interests.

Because make no mistake: Sponsors, unlike mentors, *really need* you. They need your support and skills. They need you to build their bench strength and complement their expertise. They need you to help them realize their vision and secure their legacy. You advance their careers, surprising as that might seem. There's a protégé effect akin to the sponsor effect in terms of career traction for leaders. White male leaders with a posse of protégés are 11 percent more satisfied with their own rate of advancement than leaders who haven't invested in up-and-comers. Leaders of color who've developed young talent are overall 24 percent more satisfied with their career progress than those who haven't built that base of support.

THE TWO-WAY STREET IN ACTION: ROSALIND HUDNELL AND JANE SHAW

The moment she joined the guests gathered for Intel Chairwoman Jane Shaw's retirement dinner, Rosalind Hudnell knew she had arrived.

Virtually all of them were board members. She was one of only three guests who weren't part of that inner circle. Yet with every executive she met, Hudnell felt tacit acknowledgment that she *belonged*. Clearly, Shaw's inclusion of her implied that. But it was what Shaw's invitation acknowledged: not just her seventeen years of service to the company as a diversity officer, but the respect she had acquired for her contribution to Shaw's personal legacy, which was to advance women onto corporate boards worldwide.

Their relationship had begun when Shaw, poised to make a speech on the role of quotas in boosting women's

(continued)

board participation, sought out Hudnell for advice: Given her experience as a diversity chief, what did she believe her [Shaw's] message should be? "We worked really well together and I was honored to be asked to help her find her voice on this critical issue," Hudnell recalls. From then on, Hudnell acted as a vital sounding board for her sponsor, helping her vet high-visibility projects. "Jane relied on me because she trusted I knew the subject matter and what she could achieve," Hudnell observes.

More critically, Hudnell began to connect Shaw with people who could provide the forums she sought. "One of the things Jane absolutely loved was the depth of my network, the genuine relationships I'd cultivated with people," she observed. "Every place I brought her to, she'd walk away thinking, 'Wow, that wouldn't have happened without Roz.' I mean, here was this incredibly influential woman, a leader of companies, who was relatively unknown on the outside. I was proud to help change that."

What surprised Hudnell about the invitation to Shaw's board retirement dinner was that she never thought of Shaw as her sponsor. In hindsight, she now realizes it was a tremendous moment of sponsorship. "I want you to know Roz Hudnell," Shaw said, introducing her last among her guests that evening, "because the work she and I have done around women and diversity is the work

I'm most proud of." Shaw went on to talk about what she had witnessed with the high esteem others accorded her everywhere she traveled. "I want you to continue to give Roz your full support," Shaw concluded, "because the work she is doing is vital to Intel's success."

That was in May 2012. In early 2013, when Roz and I spoke, she had just been promoted to vice president one of only 140 such officers worldwide in a company of nearly 100,000.

Of course, Roz hastens to point out, Jane wasn't the only one who stepped in to help her realize her leadership potential at Intel. Carlene Ellis, the firm's first female executive, had played a seminal role when Roz first arrived, making sure she won important audiences for her viewpoint. And Richard Taylor, senior vice president of human resources, had provided her with key opportunities to take on visible assignments, including putting her in charge of CEO Paul Otellini's involvement with President Obama's Council on Jobs & Competitiveness and championing her VP nomination. And finally, Otellini himself had been the executive champion for diversity. "He supported my ideas, backed me up with the senior leadership team, and ultimately was the one who appointed me vice president," Roz told me.

(*continued*)

But it was through Jane that Roz saw her career culminate in an acceptance beyond what dogged effort and sterling credentials could ever alone have earned her. "Being invited to that event, being included in something that intimate, and feeling so at ease in a room of such power—it was the moment you always dream of when you know you've finally arrived," Roz relates, "where you don't have to prove you belong anymore." That's what Jane's advocacy has done for her, she says: "She provided me with such validation—and by doing it in front of her peers it was a moment for me that was so personally powerful."

She reflected a moment and then added, "Now is my opportunity to stay committed to make sure that I can be in a position to do that for another deserving person in the future."

Just how important protégés are to their sponsors was made clear in a conversation I had with a *Fortune* 100 CEO. He told me that when he does that final interview with an executive at his company who is being considered for a promotion to the C-suite, he asks the all-important question: "How many people do you have in your pocket?" What he means by this, he explained, is "How many talented young people have you sponsored over the years—people who now hold key positions in this company—so that if I asked you to do something impossible next week that involved liaising across seven geographies and five functions, you could pull it off? How many leaders out there 'owe you one,' think you're wonderful, and would give huge priority to your project?" Fundamentally, he told me, "I'm not interested in anyone who doesn't have deep pockets."

So have that bench strength and you will go far, as far as you make clear you want to go (you need a destination in mind, as discussed in part II). Don't wait to be tapped for special projects or asked to assume a leadership role. Act like a leader, and leaders will take you under their wings. Show vision, and visionaries will invite you to do more of it. The power to work the levers rests squarely in your hands. As with Dorothy and her ruby slippers, unleashing the magic depends on first realizing that you already have what you need to get back to Kansas . . . or start your own company . . . or break through to the next big job . . . or fulfill your vision for social justice. With that realization, it's then only a matter of making the journey. I'm going to help you every step of the way. Turn to the map in part II, and let's get started.

PART TWO

Road Map for Protégés

- Embrace your dream and do a diagnostic

- Scan the horizon for potential sponsors

- Distribute your risk

- Understand that it's not all about you

- Come through on two obvious fronts

- Develop and deploy your currency

- Lean in and lead with a yes

3

Embrace Your Dream and Do a Diagnostic

D o you have a vision for yourself? A clear picture of your career destination? Do you know what success—*your* success—will look and feel like?

Executive coach Gail Blanke suggests that anyone contemplating an arduous undertaking remember Walt Disney's advice to the executives planning the Magic Kingdom: *build the castle first*. Back in 1971 when he was spearheading that first theme park, he understood that everyone involved in achieving his dream—from the Madison Avenue ad men selling it to the guys hacking their way through the mosquito-infested Florida swamp—needed literally to see the majesty and the beauty of this vision, lest they forget what they were working toward. So the first thing to rear up out of the Orlando swamp was, in fact, Disney's castle, which, with its fluttering flags and soaring gilded turrets, was the very embodiment of the magic he intended to make. It worked wonders, lifting morale, enhancing performance. As Blanke observes, "Nothing really big, really bold, or really beautiful was ever created in a country, in a company, in a family, or in a life without a *vision*—a vision so powerful that people will work miracles to bring it to life."

The Vision Thing

Building a successful career is one tough journey. No matter who you are, no matter where you're coming from, and no matter what you bring to the undertaking, you need a vision: not just a goal, but a dream; not just a destination, but an inspiration. A good sense of direction and loads of drive will serve you well, but you've got to see where you're headed to set a course and be hugely motivated by what you see in order to push forward. With a magnificent castle beckoning on the horizon, you can fend off swarms of mosquitoes and keep lifting your feet out of the muck.

The vision thing, however, is where women falter. They set out with a purpose, but not a dream. They are committed and driven, yet hesitant to put their foot down on the gas and keep it there. As Sheryl Sandberg, COO of Facebook, points out in her new book *Lean In*, it's as though they're driving with one foot on the brake, holding back in tiny but impactful ways from the get-go, pruning their career plans to accommodate marriage and children long before they're even in a relationship. Rather than build their castle and strive to inhabit it, they tentatively sign on to an arduous journey and hope their slog will deliver them someplace sometime.

What accounts for this ambivalence, this seeming failure of vision? There are three things going on here.

For starters, women continue to have more distractions than men. For two decades, they have toddlers or teenagers nipping at their heels, and no matter what their child-care arrangements, that's a significant preoccupation (as is the ticking biological clock that precedes these decades). They're also still burdened with more than their fair share on the home front (our research shows that 56 percent of working women shoulder 75 percent of the child care, and 60 percent do 75 percent of the chores). Taken together, the second and third shift at home mean that, at work, women simply don't have the "white space," or unencumbered time, to do some blue-sky thinking about who they want to be, what they want to do, and where they want to end up.

Then there's the ongoing lack of compelling role models. Few female leaders provide an image of success women can really embrace. If they happen to be world leaders (think Condoleezza Rice) or monumentally successful business-women (think Oprah Winfrey), then we're obliged to dwell on what they *don't* have—the missing life partner, the nonexistent offspring—that we're just not prepared to sacrifice ourselves. Older women in particular throw into relief the awful bargain that ambitious women must seemingly strike—the kind of glaring sacrifice men just don't have to make. If somehow a woman does win the triple crown—career, spouse, children— we hold against her the sacrifices we feel *aren't* being made but should be. Remember how Hillary Clinton was pilloried for taking command and control of the health-care bill during her stint as First Lady? And how, at the same time, her cookie-baking prowess came under scrutiny? Implicit in the attacks was the suggestion that by driving a pivotal piece of legislation, she was shortchanging her husband and child and, indeed, the nation, as White House wife and mother.

The other reality is that amazingly capable women who do make it to a career pinnacle rarely talk about the agency, impact, influence, and joy that come with their achievement. Instead they talk about sacrifice and struggle. Looking back, I'm at fault myself. I'm sure that during the years I was coping with difficult childbearing experiences (I miscarried twins and subsequently gave birth to an extremely premature child), I failed to fully "share" with students and colleagues the enormous satisfaction I derived from publishing my first book or giving my first keynote address. But my voice was inconsequential. Women who have real power bear a particular responsibility to talk eloquently, openly, and frequently about the fruits of success. Consider Anne-Marie Slaughter's piece in the October 2012 issue of the *Atlantic Monthly*.[1] In this poignant article (which went viral and was read by millions), she chooses to focus not on the magic of her dream job (she headed up policy planning at the US State Department), but on the unexpectedly fierce tugs and pulls exerted by her teenage son back home in Princeton. With searing honesty she walks us through just how difficult it had become to "do the kind of job I wanted to do as a high government official and be the kind of parent I wanted to be, at a demanding time for my children." As I read the article I wanted her to also paint a rich and alluring portrait of how wonderful it was to have impact and agency in Washington. What did it feel like to shape foreign policy at a watershed moment in history—when American power in the world was newly projected by an African American president and a female secretary of state? Now that role and position might be worth sacrifice and struggle.

In other words, female ambition is laced with ambivalence because every fluttering flag women see on the horizon bespeaks of a burning castle, a success not worth attaining at the price it will extort. Younger women, fearful that too much success will scare off eligible men, scale back their castle and embark on their careers with one foot on the brake. More-senior women, unwilling to uproot and relocate their families should they be selected for a regional directorship, duck below the radar of the search committee or succession planners. They're not afraid of hard work, but they most certainly fear what hard work will net them in the way of greater visibility, accountability, and time away from their families. That a top job might endow them with significant autonomy, or grant their children singular opportunities, or position them to effect sweeping change for all women seems not to hold much sway in their calculus. They're focused strictly on the cost.

This gloomy state of affairs needn't persist. Facebook's Sheryl Sandberg, Yahoo's Marissa Mayer, and US Senator Elizabeth Warren are already changing the conversation, showing that women can not only win the triple crown, but also revel in its spoils. Some of these voices—Cherie Blair, Joanna Coles, and Sallie Krawcheck, for example—you'll find in this book. In the final chapter, I'll share my own castle and describe how I dreamed it and what I feel about it now that I inhabit it. That should get you thinking about a bold and beautiful vision for your own success. This is the first step in your journey.

JOANNA COLES

You've likely seen her on TV, on CBS playing herself as the formidable editor in chief of *Cosmopolitan*, or in her mentor role on *Project Runway All Stars*, judging the career prospects of aspiring fashion designers. Or maybe you caught one of her many appearances on national news programs including *Anderson Cooper 360*, *CBS This Morning*, and MSNBC's *Morning Joe*.

Ever since 2011, when *Adweek* named her "Editor of the Year" in recognition of the extraordinary job she'd done at *Marie Claire*, Joanna Coles has been seizing the national spotlight—the very embodiment of the *Cosmo* girl with her chic looks and cheeky professionalism.

And she's clearly loving every minute.

"I didn't realize, before I became editor in chief of *Marie Claire*, how much I was going to enjoy being in charge," she says.

Since September 2012, when I interviewed her, Joanna's been in charge of *Cosmopolitan*, the world's largest women's magazine with sixty-four international editions and best-selling digital and newsstand versions. The job entails much more than overseeing content for the print magazine: there is also the website, tablet, and brand extensions, including *Cosmo Radio* on Sirius/XM, the Cosmopolitan Collection of lingerie, handbags, and shoes at JCPenney, and even a joint venture with Harlequin Books. Yet when we spoke, she wasn't the least bit stressed. On the contrary, this is the level of command she's sought her entire life.

"I love seeing my ideas of what a magazine for women should be unfold, and watching them take shape over a number of issues. It's thrilling being the person ultimately making the decisions."

(continued)

She knows only too well the frustrations of being number two—the role she played at *More* magazine prior to taking over at *Marie Claire* in 2006. "I would be consulted, of course, and would give my opinion—it might be the choice of cover art or the mix of features within the magazine," she explains. "But in the end it wasn't my decision and I would often disagree. You yearn to play out your own vision."

In her six-year tenure at *Marie Claire*, that vision played out in extraordinary ways. For two years running, the magazine was nominated for public service awards for its investigative journalism. One story on buried rape kits—evidence victims submitted to police that was subsequently ignored—got the magazine shortlisted for an award that ultimately was conferred on *The New Yorker*. "Just the fact we were up there alongside a storied magazine with a huge tradition of investigative journalism made me so proud," she told me. "Traditionally, women's magazines are not in this territory."

Coles's vision also proved remarkably successful in terms of ad revenues, which she boosted by 31 percent over the course of 2011. With 181 pages of glossy, high-end advertisements from the likes of Gucci and Bulgari, the spring 2012 issue broke a record in the magazine's seventeen-year history. Newsstand sales rose, too, despite the downward trend in print media overall and the sluggish economy.

Many former journalists would find that kind of success stressful. But Coles, who used to chase down everyone from politicians to criminals to file stories for *The Guardian* and the *Times of London*, finds her high-visibility job at the helm "hugely liberating." What produces stresses and strains, she told me, is *not* being in control of your schedule, especially if you're a parent and are tugged and pulled by responsibilities to children. She remembers with painful clarity a hellish week that began on the morning of her son's second birthday. Her editor at the *Times* called to have her cover a breaking story about two professors who'd been stabbed at Dartmouth College in New Hampshire. She told him she couldn't do it; he called back and told her he really needed her to do this. So she handed the birthday boy to her husband who had just arrived home from a business trip, traveled to Dartmouth, and set about capturing the story—interviewing neighbors, hiring a photographer, and staying up until 5:00 a.m. to meet the deadline. And then her editor called to say that, as much as everyone loved the story, they weren't going to run it until the end of the week.

(continued)

"That was the moment I realized these two lifestyles are no longer compatible," she said. "Here I'd just missed my son's second birthday for a story that didn't run. I knew what my priorities were: I wanted to work and I wanted to have a family. But I needed more control and the impetus was on me to go find it."

Finding the right job wasn't easy. Coles took an editing job at *New York Magazine*, as it seemed to offer, with more regular hours, more control. Instead, she found herself working until 11 p.m. three days a week, and going home to a "second shift" (she often was up all night with her newborn). "It was the only time I've understood what it must be like to be a drug addict," she said. "I would get up in the morning and all I could think about was when I could get more sleep, how I could get more sleep, I have to get more sleep. If someone could have given me an intravenous drip of sleep, I would have taken it. I was desperate. Those three years were really tough."

But she powered through, sustained by her belief that she would "eventually run the show." When she got the job heading up *Marie Claire*, she at last had the control—over her schedule and over the strategic vision of the magazine—she had sought throughout her career. "I suppose this boils down to power," she commented, "but that's not how I thought about it at the time. I saw it as the ability to drive the right decisions in areas of life that I cared about most."

In addition to her role at *Cosmopolitan*, Coles derives enormous joy and satisfaction in being at the red-hot center of the fashion world. For two seasons prior to taking over the magazine, she starred in *Project Runway All Stars*, the spin-off of *Project Runway* that she helped create with *Marie Claire* fashion director Nina Garcia. Fashion allows her, she says, a unique perk: to be celebratory about the place she's in and the living she earns. She laments that women cannot talk about money without seeming "braggy"—and unlikeable. "It's increasingly important to earn your own money," she observes. "It buys you freedom from a miserable relationship. It buys you freedom from bosses you're no longer in sync with. Being on edge financially is very stressful. It undermines your energy." She adds, "These are things we women don't talk about enough."

Dare to Dream

So you're going to dream, and you're going to dream big. You're going to embrace your God-given right to power, influence, agency, and impact. You're going to own your ambition, and you're going to design a castle for it, right here and now. Because without a clear sense of your destination, there's no point in getting yourself a sponsor. Sponsors are the dream enablers.

To get started with this dream work, consider the following questions:

- What place would feel magical? What kind of room or space do you want to inhabit? What is the view when you look out the window?

- Whom do you want to meet with? Who intrigues you or excites you? What sort of conversation do you wish you could have with them?

- What transformation do you most want to drive? What sort of large-scale change do you wish you could be part of?

These are challenging questions, which is why women put them off. But if you give yourself permission to contemplate any and all answers—if you don't burden the process by trying to be realistic or pragmatic, if you forget the "should" and don't think about the "cans"—this exercise can be incredibly liberating and inspiring. If it's not, or you're having trouble silencing that ever-rational left brain, turn to the epilogue. You might well benefit, too, from consulting the vast tranche

of motivational literature, including Gail Blanke's bc
Throw Out Fifty Things: Clear the Clutter, Find Your Life.[2]

Just commit to building *a* castle, if not *the* castle.
Understand you are not going to make any more excuses or
tolerate any more postponements. No matter how old you
are, you simply don't have time. None of us do. There will
be plenty of detours and side railings without you furnishing
your own at the very start.

Do a Diagnostic

Now you can get pragmatic: with those turrets and flags fluttering on the horizon, you can determine what you've got in
your kit that will help you attain your dream.

Assess what you *have*: what you've done, what you've
proven you can do, what you're ready to do again. Resist
the temptation to catalog skills you don't have, or feel you
should have by now, or are afraid you'll never have. Catalog
only your strengths. It's essential you answer the following
questions:

- What do you do exceptionally well? In what skill sets
  do you have your black belt?

- What is your currency? What sets you apart?

- What experiences distinguish you?

- What inherent or acquired differences lend you a distinctive brand or value added that others may not bring to the table?

- What accomplishment has given you joy and won you accolades? What gives you satisfaction so you want to do more of it?

- How does the mission or mandate of your organization overlap with your own values or goals?

This is heavy lifting, but you needn't do it alone. This work is ideal to take up with a mentor. Mentors have the time and the inclination to help you with your self-assessment as well as your blue-sky thinking. A selfless desire to help you with your future is what makes them mentors. They can see and put into words what you may not see about yourself or be able to articulate. You might also consult online assessment tools and any performance reviews that have been done on you at work (if you've not been evaluated, now's the time to make that request). Classes, seminars, or lectures are other good opportunities to hold a mirror to yourself or discover what you didn't know about your abilities. Remember, the inventory you want to take is strictly positive.

CHERIE BLAIR

To most Americans, Cherie Blair is a Famous Wife—the spouse of ex-Prime Minister Tony Blair and mother of his four children.

In fact, there is another Cherie: Cherie Booth QC, as she is known professionally, a barrister who has achieved one of the highest honors of the legal profession as a member of the Queen's Counsel. It was Cherie, and not Tony, who first attained a coveted pupilage in the chambers of Derry Irvine, adviser to the Labor Party and Lord Chancellor for the first six years of Tony Blair's tenure as Prime Minister. Many supposed that Cherie, a blazing star in the legal profession, would enter public office ahead of Tony. "I was always interested in politics," she explains. "But I learned fairly early on that my skills as an advocate and my imagination as a lawyer were better used to achieve social change."

Booth knew firsthand the difficulties women faced if they were not allied with men. Raised by her mother and paternal grandmother—her father abandoned the family when she was a baby, and her grandfather died when she was fourteen—Booth excelled at school, earning a First class degree at the London School of

Economics and winning the prize for top student. She was top-of-her-class on the bar exams, as well. When she went to get a job as a lawyer, however, she found that being a wife and mother were the only identities others perceived. "Suddenly I learned the reality of the world in the 1970s: that women still should know their place," she comments. "The assumption was that backing a woman wasn't a good idea because obviously, she would leave."

Booth did not leave. Through the births of three of her children, she committed herself to challenging cases in employment and discrimination law, a brand-new field in which she was ideally credentialed. The cases she took on—arguing on behalf of a Muslim schoolgirl who wanted to wear a hijab to school, on behalf of a lesbian who sued South-West trains for denying concessions to her partner, and seeking damages for a girl whose school failed to diagnose her dyslexia—established her as a formidable voice in social justice and a viable contender for the Queen's Counsel.

Soon after the birth of her third child in 1988, Booth decided to move chambers (the UK equivalent of changing law firms) in order to position herself for her QC bid, approaching one of the firms who'd turned her down when she was seeking her first position as a barrister—"quite a hard thing, a masculine thing, for me to do," she notes. In addition to her caseload, Booth was involved in the bar's council, chaired the bar's IT committee, and was mounting a bid for Queen Counsel, all while her husband was campaigning to lead the Labor Party. The day she heard she'd been appointed QC turned out to be, coincidentally, the very day she and her husband were invited to dine with the Queen. "It's quite rare for a QC to be able actually to thank the Queen personally for being appointed," Booth notes. "It was a fantastic moment. I felt I had achieved something truly significant by dint of my own efforts and abilities." She was the seventy-sixth woman in Britain's history to "take silk," a reference to the gown that QC barristers wear in court. At forty-one years old, she was by far the youngest.

Booth has acquired many accolades since then. Today, she's recognized globally for her ongoing human rights advocacy, particularly on behalf of women. Indeed, her work spearheading the Cherie Blair Foundation for Women, which has improved the earning power and life prospects of twenty thousand women worldwide, won her a CBE in the January 2013 honors list. "Having financial independence has given me a voice; other women should be able to have that voice, too," she says. "It's fantastic to think I have done something to help them."

(continued)

But to this day, she regards the QC ceremony as her crowning achievement. The photos capture some of the pomp: the long, full-bodied wig, the elaborate lace ruffle, the pair of breeches she had specially made in lieu of the skirt her predecessors had been made to wear. Nor will she ever forget piling into a Rolls-Royce with her children, being driven to Westminster Hall in Parliament, and being greeted by the clerk in his gloves and morning suit. "It's a very old ritual," she explains. "The Lord Chancellor makes a speech about the importance of the legal system and, one by one, all the new silks take an oath of allegiance to the Queen. After that you're called to the Lord Chief Justice's court, the highest judge in the land, where you move to the outer bar. In my year it was a particularly big event, not because of me (though there was a lot of press because I was the Leader of the Opposition's wife) but because six women were appointed, the most ever."

With her sister and mother in attendance, Booth was especially conscious of the three generations of dreams she carried that day. "What was going through my head was how proud my mum was, and how proud my grandmother would have been," she recalls. "From a very early age my grandmother had been a huge fan of

Rose Heilbron—the first female silk—because Heilbron was, like her, from Liverpool. My grandmother used to go and watch her plead in court. I don't think that in all those years when she was such a big fan of Rose's that she ever thought her granddaughter would become Heilbron's successor. That day at Westminster gave me a huge sense of accomplishment and gratitude. It was a pretty big thing for a working-class girl from Liverpool to have done."

Assess Your Organization

Having a confident handle on what you bring to the mission is half the diagnostic. The other half is assessing the context in which you'll be leveraging those strengths. You must map the organizational landscape. Consider the following questions:

- Is your firm flat (few titles, no apparent ladder) or hierarchical? If there is a ladder, how is it constructed?

- What do titles mean in terms of what you do, where you do it, and whom you manage? Where are you on the ladder?

- If your organization is flat and titles mean nothing, how do you then navigate the organization?

- What deliverables will get you promoted? As I discovered as a young professor, being "teacher of the year" was certainly an indication of high performance, but it did not win me tenure. Nor did publishing a high-impact trade book. Publication in obscure but highly regarded, peer-reviewed journals was the deliverable I should have focused on.

- What are the notch points—the sticky places, the plateaus, dips, or pitfalls—you need to power through? Every company, every profession, every worthwhile journey has these shoals, and many capable employees have foundered on them. Identify them now so that when you do win a sponsor, you know where to focus his or her efforts.

Again, for help with this homework, turn to mentors. A well-chosen mentor will know the lay of the land in your firm. More importantly, he or she has successfully navigated it. Mentors can help you understand the unwritten rules, provide a map for the uncharted corridors to power, and reveal the business behind the business. They are typically

not positioned to make your dream happen, nor d
owe you that kind of leg up. But in assisting you wit
essential assessment, they prepare you to attract sponsors.

Nail the Tactics

- Look for role models. Read about people (like
  Coles and Booth) whose achievements inspire
  you. Keep refreshing your pool. It's important you
  have a robust sampling, lest the daily cavalcade of
  stories about unrewarded struggle or unwarranted
  sacrifice succeed in dampening your drive. Amazing
  people triumph, often overcoming hurdles far
  greater than your own. Put them in your sights.

- Envisage yourself at age fifty, with twenty-five
  productive years ahead of you. It's never too late to
  focus on a goal and go after it.

- Consult with a mentor, role model, or personal
  development coach who can help you see the
  big picture. Brainstorm a professional target list.
  Write down your aspirations, however modest
  or fabulous, and figure out how to hold yourself
  accountable.

- If you've had your performance assessed using an industry diagnostic (a Hogan Personality Inventory or 360-degree review, for example), ask for the results and review them with your manager and/or mentor to zero in on your strengths. If you haven't had a performance review, informal or formal, ask for one. No matter what size company you work for, somebody's taking your measure. Don't miss out on the opportunity to benefit from their perspective.

4

Scan the Horizon for
Potential Sponsors

Fourteen years ago, Audrey was toiling in the trenches as one among a legion of junior-level project managers in the National Australia Group's Glasgow office. Intent on relocating, she had set her sights on Melbourne, Australia, because only a handful of UK expats ever got to work in Australia, and she wanted that breadth of experience on her résumé. "I knew it would powerfully accelerate my career," she explains.

She also knew she would need help: some powerful executive who would talk glowingly about her skill sets, lobby for her relocation, and ensure that other candidates didn't beat her to the finish line. She needed a sponsor.

Scanning the office for candidates—leaders who knew her but who also had pull in the Australian office—Audrey targeted a senior executive, an Australian expatriate who had worked in the UK for five years but was due to return home within the year. She had the perfect entrée with him: he'd asked her to oversee a twelve-month project for him. She also had what struck her as ideal leverage: three other executives had also come to her with projects they wanted her to manage ("I'd waited for a bus and suddenly four showed up," she notes), and she had to choose. So she shared with him her conundrum about whom to work for, sketched for him her long-range plan, and proposed a quid pro quo: she'd take on his project if he'd agree to advocate for her transfer to the Melbourne office. "My approach wasn't, 'Oh, would you sponsor me,'" Audrey explained, "but more along the lines of, 'If I turn down these options and do a great job for you on your project, would you commit to helping me get a job in Australia?'"

He signed on.

The project lasted about twelve months. That was fine with Audrey, who had just begun the course work for an MBA. During that time, her sponsor returned to Australia, with a reminder from Audrey not to forget to look for opportunities for her. "We agreed that he needed to get settled back home and have some time to dig down into his job and new network, because you can't be an effective sponsor unless you have that," she explained. So her sponsor spent the next year establishing himself in his new life and his new executive job. Audrey spent it doing a splendid job on the project he had asked her to take on, while wrapping up her MBA. To underscore her commitment to the bank (and make herself more valuable), Audrey had paid for her MBA herself. As a show of good faith, her sponsor persuaded the bank to reimburse her for her tuition fees. It proved, for both parties, an excellent investment. Audrey missed her graduation, as she was in Melbourne celebrating her new job: head of strategy for global shared services in Australia.

Sponsors versus Supporters

Is there someone in your corner? How do you know?

In our survey research, we asked employees if they had sponsors. Over 40 percent of our respondents—men and women, Caucasian and multicultural professionals—said yes. While not a majority, this number nonetheless surprised us. If so many already had the backing of senior leaders, why did so few of these employees actually progress into leadership?

The truth became apparent in the follow-up question we posed. We asked, *Which of the following does your sponsor do for you?* We listed key deliverables (see the definition of a sponsor in chapter 2). The number of respondents who had sponsors plummeted. Forced to discern between sideline cheerleaders and center-ring champions, a mere 13 percent of female professionals and a paltry 8 percent of non-Caucasian employees laid claim to real champions—leaders who expended chips on their behalf, advocated for the next promotion, and provided air cover.

The fact is, few women and professionals of color differentiate between supporters and true sponsors.

Turbocharging Support into Sponsorship

Some supporters, including mentors, can be converted into effective sponsors. It's a matter of taking an existing relationship and making it instrumental. But it's up to you to initiate that conversion.

Start by identifying would-be sponsors among your supporters. Good bets will be leaders who (1) are already aware of your skills and strengths, (2) stand to benefit from your help, and (3) have the clout to move you toward your goal, whatever that may be. Consider who knows you and knows of your work, or has heard about you and your work. Consider not whom you report to, but whom your boss reports to. In a large organization, look for someone two bandwidths away. In a small firm, seize on someone who's got the principal's ear but doesn't stand between you and your goal. If you're on your own, as a sole proprietor or freelancer, target in client organizations who could evangelize on your behalf with those people in their network who make the hiring decisions.

Now look for telltale, sponsorlike behaviors. If you've won a piece of business or been assigned to a special project, who was responsible for the decision? If you were invited to a meeting you wouldn't normally attend or given an unsolicited contact, who issued the invitation? You'll know a potential sponsor by his or her actions, which include connecting you to key people or clients, giving you stretch assignments, offering critical feedback, and promoting your visibility within the firm or within their networks.

Once you've homed in on a would-be sponsor, do not ask for sponsorship. Rather, show what makes you worth sponsoring or describe what you can bring to his or her team or project. You may want to take Audrey's tack: propose a quid pro quo. Turning a supporter into an advocate depends on your clarifying what makes you a good investment, what you're willing to do for that person, and what help you'd like in return. If this sounds blatantly transactional, okay, it is. But remember, truly powerful people simply don't have the time to divine what makes you tick or what will make you happy. You owe it to both of you to cut to the chase, not in making demands, but in spelling out the mutual benefits.

Jolie learned this the hard way. As a pharmacist without a medical degree working at a firm where every top leader had one, Jolie knew she'd need some powerful support to get promoted. When she found a senior (male) executive willing to meet with her regularly, she thought she'd found her lever.

"I remember having a conversation with him about women in science who didn't have an MD," Jolie recalled. "I asked him what they'd have to do to show they had the experience, if not the credentials, to move up in this firm. And the whole time we're talking, I'm thinking, 'I'll forge a relationship, then he'll be in position to say good things about me, and I'll get a bigger job.' I thought that's how it would work."

Nothing happened.

Jolie reconsidered her tactic. "I had this incredible 'aha!' moment," she explained. "I realized, for starters, that this guy was way too high up for me to be going to him to work out an issue. That was a waste of his time and my opportunity. Then I realized he couldn't push for my promotion if he didn't know what I was doing. Here I'd been meeting with him quarterly for over a year, chatting about this and that, when I should really have been helping him understand the work that I did and what I had accomplished. Finally, I realized I needed to show him what I had to offer him in terms of skills and expertise he could use on the projects he was trying to push forward."

Today, she reports to that executive—and she's the only person on the team who doesn't have a medical degree.

Target the Ones with Juice

Wilma, a rising star in American Express's mergers and acquisitions division in New York, participates in two mentoring programs. Every quarter she meets with a cluster of mentees and mentors as part of a national initiative dedicated to pairing female executives from various industry sectors with high-potential women who, like Wilma, are poised to break through to senior management in historically male-dominated industries. And every month she meets one-on-one with Connie, a former executive vice president at a global financial services firm and a tireless champion of working mothers who had herself negotiated a flextime arrangement, working out of her home in Scarsdale, New York, to oversee operations in India.

Connie is unquestionably Wilma's role model as well as mentor. She's a stalwart friend, too. But a senior leader best positioned to get Wilma promoted to her dream job of heading up M&A at corporate headquarters?

Probably not.

When scanning your horizon for would-be sponsors (yes, you'll need more than one), bear in mind that the best candidates are very likely *not* going to be people with whom you'd want to share your innermost secrets. They may not even be leaders you hugely admire. Rather, the best candidates are people in a position to get you where you're keen on going—people inside or outside your company who have clout in the circle you aspire to join or influence in the community you're eager to embrace. If they happen to be leaders you like, if they happen to have a management style you wish to emulate, so much the better. But do not attempt to convert mentors or role models who don't have—and never will have—"the juice" into sponsors. It won't work. I discovered this the hard way when I ended up sponsorless at Barnard College despite my friendship with the likes of Annette Baxter, a luminary in her field but powerless at my institution.

Our data and our interviews show that many high-potential women make the mistake of aligning themselves with role models rather than powerfully positioned sponsors. Indeed, 42 percent of our female survey respondents say they are looking for sponsorship from collaborative, inclusive leaders, because that style of leadership is one they embody or hope to emulate. The problem is that most leaders with juice—the ones who have the power to lever promising women into the topmost band—aren't inclusive collaborators. Only 28 percent of men and women at US companies say this is the dominant style of leadership at their firm. Nearly twice as many—45 percent of survey respondents—say that the most prevalent kind is the classic, command-and-control leader who values deference from his lieutenants above all (think former GE titan Jack Welch). An additional twenty percent perceive their top management to be competitive types—hard-edged, hard-driving guys who value quarterly bottom-line results (think John Mack, Morgan Stanley storied CEO). In short, what women often value and seek in a sponsor just isn't on offer among those with real power in an organization.

This profound mismatch helps explain why so many women and people of color fail to find the real deal: sponsors who can deliver. They align themselves with people whom they trust and like or who, they believe, trust and like them. CTI survey data affirm this: women and multicultural professionals look for someone "whose leadership style I admire" (with 56 percent of women and 52 percent of multicultural professionals in accord). As a result, they're less inclined, at critical stages, to align their interests with people who can turbocharge their prospects and forge strategic alliances. As one woman ruefully explained to me, "I've wasted ten years impressing the wrong people."

So when you're eyeing your galaxy of supporters for would-be sponsors, seek out those with influence, power, and a voice at decision-making tables. Take a page out of Sheryl Sandberg's playbook: early in the game—while she was still an undergraduate at Harvard—Sandberg sought to impress Lawrence Summers, an academic powerhouse. He made her his research assistant and when he was subsequently tapped to run the World Bank, he brought Sandberg with him as his research analyst. When he moved over to the US Treasury, Sandberg (who was twenty-nine years old) became his chief of staff. Summers, who is perhaps best known for pointing out that women lack the intellectual wattage to be the world's top scientists, was probably not a role model Sandberg hoped to emulate. But did he have juice? Oceans of it.

And once you've found these people, get yourself in front of them. This may require extraordinary measures. I have in mind my friend Joanna Coles who, as a senior editor at *More* magazine, set her sights on a bigger role at Hearst, its parent company. Coles determined she needed to meet with Cathie Black, then CEO of Hearst and a powerhouse in the media industry. Coles managed, after considerable persistence, to get a meeting scheduled with Black. The morning of the meeting, she got a call from Black's office saying that the meeting would have to be canceled, as Black was heading to the airport to attend a board meeting. Undeterred, Coles told Black's assistant she would share the ride to JFK Airport with Black. She hopped in a cab, got to Black's office just as the limo was leaving, joined Black in the back seat, and spent the next forty minutes in conversation with her target sponsor. Today, as we know, Coles is editor in chief of *Cosmopolitan* magazine.

Nail the Tactics

- Choose your targets carefully.

  - Put efficacy over affinity. Role models are great to have, but they may not make effective sponsors.

— Don't be put off by leadership style. You need to respect your sponsor, not vow to become him or her. Your target may exercise authority in a way you don't care to copy, but it's his clout, not his style, that will turbocharge your career.

— Friends don't make the best sponsors. Doubtless you have friends; what you need in a sponsor is a strategic ally. Friendship can actually hinder a relationship that's instrumental in nature.

— By all means impress your boss, but seek as your sponsor someone with the power to change your career. Would-be sponsors in large organizations are ideally two levels above you, with line of sight into your performance and your career. In smaller firms, either they're the founder or president, or they have the ear of that person.

• Get in front of would-be sponsors.

— Ask a supportive manager for stretch assignments in your target sponsor's line of sight.

— Request a meeting with your target sponsor for career development advice.

— Attend networking events, conferences, and extracurricular or informal gatherings where you might have occasion to approach your target and introduce yourself. Be able to articulate not just who you are and what you do but your distinct value added—the hook that will spark interest and ensure you're remembered as someone who has something to offer, rather than as someone who's making a demand.

— Approach a target sponsor and suggest collaborating on a project of interest to that person. "Be super-prepared and go out of your way to make clear how much you plan on helping out with number-crunching and legwork as well new ideas," says Columbia's Katherine Phillips. "You'll be surprised at how well you'll be received, as most leaders—whatever the field or sector—are looking for ways to stay on the cutting edge, and many of them struggle with huge time constraints. Coleading a project or coauthoring an article with an eminence can make all the difference to your career."

— Propose a quid pro quo. Identify ways you might help your sponsor solve a looming business challenge. Offer to contribute in a concrete way. At the same time, explain what you are looking for in the way of advocacy: introductions to other department heads, stretch opportunities within your own division, lateral moves to gain experience or promotions. Suggest that an alliance can work to your mutual benefit.

— If your target sponsor demurs, ask if he or she can direct you to a more appropriate leader. Ask if he or she will introduce you.

5

Distribute Your Risk

Let's say you have a sponsor, someone who's taken an interest in you, gone out on a limb for you, lobbied for your promotion, and provided you with air cover so that you can take risks and burnish both of your brands. If tomorrow this person left the company, could you survive and thrive?

Leadership churn is something Gabriella, a thirty-four-year-old cable television producer, knows something about. Two years ago, with her reputation soaring thanks to signing a big-name talent, Gabriella was handed a wonderful stretch role: producing a prime-time reality show. Her long-time sponsor, Toni, the twenty-year industry veteran who lobbied for this assignment, not only believed that Gabriella could lead the writing team, but also that she could take a more strategic role in building the cable network's programming. "I was nervous but excited," Gabriella recalls. "I knew I'd need to impress a lot of top executives, but I felt as if Toni would have my back. I knew she wouldn't let me fail."

A year later, when a new CEO assumed the helm of the parent company, Gabriella saw a lot of those executives leave. But since Toni wasn't among them, she figured her own status was secure. "I thought, 'Okay, Toni's bulletproof, so I'm set for the long haul,'" Gabriella recalls. "I figured at her age, she wasn't going anywhere."

Then came the bombshell. A year after the CEO transition, Toni announced she was defecting to the network's biggest competitor.

Gabriella was dumbstruck. "All I could think was, 'How could she do this to me?'" Gabriella reflects. "But then I realized I might have done the same thing, had I been approached with that kind of offer at that point in my career."

Gabriella retained her position. But her influence, she feels, is on the wane. She's now a coproducer on a show that won't be renewed next season, and she's no longer invited to the strategy sessions.

"It's only been a few months, but I feel isolated and ignored," she admits. "When Toni brought me in, I saw myself becoming an executive producer before I was thirty-five. Now I feel as if I'll be lucky to keep my job."

The 2 + 1 Rule

No matter what industry you work in, no matter what job you hold, you know this: in a global economy still struggling to pull out of the 2008 financial nose dive, job insecurity is the new normal. You need a sponsor more than ever, not only to help you move up, but to help you hold on to your job. Only a powerful backer can help you keep the job you have or help you find one, should your position disappear.

As Gabriella acknowledges, however, in this economy, your sponsor is vulnerable to churn, too. We heard from a number of top-level managers who, in the wake of the 2008 collapse, found themselves out of job because they'd lost the high-level backer who might have protected them. One lamented the fact that by the time she'd realized she needed to "get a lot more intentional" about cultivating leaders as sponsors, there weren't many to be found, a phenomenon affirmed by our female survey respondents, 52 percent of whom (compared to 35 percent of the men) said that it was harder to find a sponsor due to the recession.

So you're not bulletproof, not with just one sponsor, any-way. She (or he) might be spread too thin to give you the protection you need. She might get fired. She might take a better offer elsewhere. She might peel off to launch her own venture. In short, she might well put her interests ahead of your own.

Then what?

It's not that your sponsor's departure spells the end of your relationship. Someone for whom you've worked hard, delivered results, driven revenues, or otherwise supported in measurable ways is likely to continue advocating for you. But her advocacy where you work won't be useful any longer. Unless you intend to follow her. So what to do?

The solution, of course, is to cultivate more than one sponsor, at least in a medium-sized to large firm. In organizations with fewer than ten people, you're probably best served by having one or two sponsors *outside* the firm as well as in it, in the same industry. The ideal life raft in larger organizations, CTI research shows, consists of three sponsors: two within your organization—one in your line of sight and one in a different department or division—and one outside your firm. The "2 + 1 Rule," as we call it, holds true for every career stage, from entry level to executive. One interviewee compared her sponsor strategy to her bond portfolio. "You want it diversified and you want to keep adding to it, or it won't be an adequate hedge," she counsels.

A diversified portfolio means that your sponsors should be independent of one another, so that if one goes down, the other won't go down with him or her. Yvette at Bank of America is a case in point. Yvette attained a high-visibility position in the bank's global wealth management division after the acquisition of Merrill Lynch in 2009. Because her sponsor reported directly to Sallie Krawcheck, the division's president, both Yvette and her sponsor saw their careers skyrocket during Krawcheck's impressive reign. But by 2011, Krawcheck, (despite impressive gains in her private banking division) was in the crosshairs of new CEO Brian Moynihan, whose leadership had resulted in losses of $8.8 billion for BofA during that year.[1] By September, Krawcheck was out. Yvette's sponsor was reassigned, and Yvette found herself sponsorless, too tainted by her connection with Krawcheck for anyone in the purged inner circle to extend her a lifeline. Today she works for another bank, a move that she describes as "essentially lateral" because she had to disassociate herself from her network, all of whom were in some way tied to Krawcheck. "We all lost ground because we'd hitched ourselves to Sallie," she told me in our interview.

Building your portfolio of sponsors means increasing the number of arenas in which you play a leadership role. Your job isn't a big enough stage to put you on the radar of powerful individuals outside your team, department, or division. If you work for a large company, as many of our focus group participants do, volunteer for formal mentoring programs *as a mentor*, because a conspicuous role in any leadership development program invariably makes you visible to a wide range of high-level managers across divisions. Consider taking a leading role in an employee network or affinity group. If you're not already participating, here's a perfect example of why to get involved. Barbara Adachi, head of human capital for Deloitte Consulting

LLP, talks about "finding" both of her protégés through WIN, Deloitte's initiative to retain and advance women, which Adachi led from 2007–2012. It was their offer to help her and their follow-through on the important tasks she assigned them that won them her advocacy. "Even though one of my protégés was in another practice, I was able to be a voice at the table when she came up for promotion to partner," Adachi says. After twenty years, WIN is now embedded in Deloitte's culture and advancing women is a leadership priority.

For that external sponsor, you need to cultivate vibrant networks outside work. Join a philanthropic cause, get on a nonprofit board, take a leadership role in your church or synagogue, or head up your alumni chapter, all with a view to gaining visibility in a larger community by demonstrating commitment and showcasing your unique skills or experience.

Deb Elam, vice president and chief diversity officer at GE, makes herself available to young talent through the National Black MBA Association and Jack and Jill of America. She's active as well on the national executive board of Delta Sigma Theta sorority and the Fairfield County chapter of The Links Inc. Elam is passionate about her causes, which give her the opportunity to leverage skills she's acquired during a twenty-five-year career at GE. They also represent an extensive network of "influentials" outside of the firm who recognize Elam as a leader.

The 2 + 1 Rule ensures you'll survive a direct hit to department, a systemic threat to your division, even a strophic blow to your firm or industry. But most importantly, it ensures you'll survive the loss of a prime sponsor. Finding and sustaining a sponsor relationship with three individuals is a daunting task, to be sure. But in these uncertain times, diversification is the name of the game.

Nail the Tactics

- Increase your internal visibility.

  - Lead a network (e.g., a women's leadership group, an African American forum) or an employee resource or affinity group.

  - Spearhead a philanthropic project, cultural event, or company sports team.

  - Ask for mentorship. Create a circle of mentors from different divisions or departments with whom you might consult on strategic shifts in your industry or career.

  - Ask your boss to introduce you to his or her boss.

  - Ask for personal development, leadership development, or formalized mentorship, as executives are often tapped to lead these internal programs.

- Increase your external visibility.

  - Join a nonprofit board relevant to your industry or sector.

  - Run for office in your professional association, community, school district, or church or synagogue.

  - Attend conferences and figure out how to be a speaker, panelist, or facilitator.

  - Create a personal board of directors or circle of mentors external to your company to get big-picture insights and advice on an optimal career path.

- Figure out the levers of power and work them.

  - Timing is everything when you think your job is under siege. Be proactive: as soon as you see the handwriting on the wall, mobilize your external as well as internal champions. When Katherine Phillips perceived that her window for tenure was shrinking at Northwestern's Kellogg School of Management, she applied for tenured positions at competitor schools and activated her network of sponsors to write her referrals. Alarmed that the competition might lure Phillips away, leaders at Kellogg swung into action and awarded her tenure. In retrospect, she sees this strategy as having given her not only tenure, but also a new confidence in her marketability.

— Change firms. The levers of power where you are may not be sufficient to boost you into the top tier. As Cherie Booth (see her story in chapter 3) notes, this takes considerable courage, fortitude, and perseverance. You may find, as she did, that the point at which a career change becomes imperative often coincides with the most intensive childbearing and childrearing years. Take a page out of her book: do your homework to determine where you need to land in order to get on track to your dreams, activate your network of sponsors outside your current company, and enlist the support of your spouse or partner. Invariably your move will require more coverage on the home front, at least while you're getting settled in your new position.

6

Understand That It's Not All About You

You're a blazing talent. You're on everyone's short list when it comes to plum assignments or missions impossible. Senior leaders want you on their team or special project. You've got a mentor. You've been given a coach. You're being tapped for leadership development.

All systems go, right?

But if for even a minute you sit back and bask in this beneficence—if you think that this attention you've been shown is all about you—then you may have already squandered your opportunity. Being a great mentee is not the skill set that will endear you to sponsors. Indeed, the mentee mind-set will cost you the support you now enjoy. It will mark you as a permanent follower.

Kelly, an EVP at a *Fortune* 500 financial services firm, tells a cautionary tale about a vice president, a direct report of hers whom she selected to advance but who failed to grasp the reciprocity of their relationship.

"I'm always looking for talent to develop, and I saw great things in him," she began, insisting I not use her name because "everyone would know" whom she was referencing. "So I put my reputation on the line and got him a role on a high-profile team in a different division where I thought he could build on his skill set, which was very complementary to mine. He was the kind of guy you could put in a room and he'd come up with the big idea, the sort of solution I would never have come up with on my own."

But then she didn't hear from him. Weeks went by. A new quarter began. Kelly had her assistant set up a face-to-face meeting with him. "He came in, sat down all relaxed. He thought we were just going to have a catch-up," she recalled. "And we were. But I laid it out for him. I said, 'You know I'm your sponsor, right?' Now he's shifting in his seat, realizing this is more than a chat. 'Yes,' he said, and thanked me. I said, 'I'm not looking for your thanks. This is mutual: we're in this together. Three, four months have gone by, and I don't know how you're performing. I have no idea if you're struggling, if you need air cover, if you need a sounding board or what.

And that's a liability for me. Because you're walking around with my brand on.'"

"He nodded, said he got it, promised he'd stay in touch," Kelly continued. "And for the next month, he did—an e-mail here and there, telling me 'Here's what I'm doing about this,' what was going well, what wasn't. He even left me cookies with a thank-you note. But then he dropped off my radar again. Shortly after I learned from a colleague that he was struggling, and his commitment to the company was on the downslope."

It was clear, as Kelly related this story, that she was still turning over what went wrong, and why. "He just didn't get the reciprocity," she reflected. "He didn't get that I needed to be kept in the loop, especially if he was in trouble, because other people were making presumptions about my eye for talent. Without regular communication, without line of sight, I couldn't manage my investment in him. I couldn't assess the risks versus the rewards of sponsoring him."

So Kelly broke off the relationship. She called a meeting, off-site, and told her erstwhile protégé that she could no longer be his sponsor and why.

"What's sad is that in the beginning, he did earn my sponsorship," Kelly observed. "He drove great results. He was a very good strategic thinker. I could put him at a table in front of anybody. I could put him in my place. And if he'd have invited me in, I could have helped him in his new role."

Shaking her head, she added, "It was very shortsighted of him not to have understood we were in this together."

Acknowledging the Pact

Sponsors may look like selfless benefactors, but they're not, not the authentic ones anyway. They can't afford to be. Given the energy that sponsorship requires and the considerable risk it entails for the sponsor, no senior leader is going to place huge bets on anybody who doesn't assure him some kind of payback. What sponsors are looking for, above all, in a protégé is someone who will deliver standout performance and be loyal and reliable.

Not every would-be protégé gets this. Neither do some would-be sponsors, according to CTI research. In our national survey, we asked managers why they cultivated protégés: was it for the benefit of the protégé or did they see the relationship benefiting themselves? Overwhelmingly, male managers—77 percent—saw it benefiting their own careers, whereas female managers—74 percent of them—assured us it was the right thing to do for the protégé's career. Men, that is, grasped the strategic value of sponsorship, whereas women saw it as mentorship writ large.

The misunderstanding stems in large part, I think, from years of mentoring initiatives. Mentoring has been hugely popular in corporate America. Human resource professionals and talent managers have seen it as something of a silver bullet for women and people of color. They craft programs, allocate budgets, engineer pairings, orchestrate meetings, and wait for the magic to happen. A 2008 Catalyst survey of full-time employees with MBAs found that 83 percent of the women and 76 percent of the men had been mentored.[1] You'd be hard-pressed these days to find a professional in middle management who hasn't been mentored to death.

Hence the mentee mind-set: a reflexive tendency to perceive any relationship with a senior person as one more piece of *your* personal development. Accustomed to the one-way flow of mentorship, promising young talent (like Kelly's protégé) approach sponsorship with the wrong assumptions and expectations. Mentees expect to be guided; they wait passively to be helped. When they're given a good steer or an open door, they perceive it as a gift rather than a debt. They persist in seeing themselves as standout performers who deserve a good turn to get them on their way, stellar employees who owe no one because they've earned their place in the sun.

It's hardly surprising, then, that Kelly's protégé "just didn't get the reciprocity." Mentoring has inculcated a culture of expectation.

You shouldn't make that mistake. Sponsors go out on a limb for someone who demonstrates she's going to go the extra mile. Sponsors advocate for someone who shows he'll continue to deliver strong results, not just for the sponsor but for the firm. Sponsors protect someone who recognizes that the sponsor's reputation is at stake. Be that someone: signal you'll be a contributor. Show you'll overdeliver. Deliver exceptional performance and prove yourself eminently trustworthy.

In the next chapter, I'll show you how.

Nail the Tactics

- Communicate.

  - Recognize when you need help and ask for it *before* you get in trouble.

  - Keep your sponsor in the loop, fully apprised of what's happening in your career (your wins and losses, triumphs, and struggles) so that he or she can offer guidance or even intervention. You are, after all, walking around with his or her brand on your forehead.

- Signal that you'll be a contributor.

  - Deliver outside your job description. Bring in some new business or win back a former client. Rainmaking may not be one of your responsibilities, but it sure will show that you are ready to assume a larger role than you currently have. One attorney described how, prior to taking maternity leave, she reached out to all the heavy hitters in her network to see if she could persuade them to bring their business to her firm. In two of three instances she hit gold, reeling in business for two partners at the firm. She was only an associate, but she wanted her bosses to see she was serious about returning and was committed to the firm. When she came back, she found she was on an accelerated partner track, thanks to having shown she would do the partners' job of building the business.

— Give what's needed without being asked. What is your sponsor working on? What's near and dear to her heart that you can help make happen? What can you take off her plate? What information do you have that she needs or that would help her do her job better? Where can you pitch in and make a difference? "If you proactively give information or do something you know will help your sponsor be successful when she doesn't ask for it," one talent professional counsels, "she'll know you have her back and are not just standing in front of her with a hand out."

— Make the small gesture. Commit random acts of everyday thoughtfulness. This could be as simple as buying an extra cappuccino at Starbucks on your way into a meeting with your sponsor. You won't appear to be a suck-up if you're someone who shows equal thoughtfulness toward your colleagues on a random, regular basis.

7

Come Through on Two
Obvious Fronts

Back in 2006, as a newly minted vice president of sales for BellSouth Advertising & Publishing, Debbie Storey contacted a colleague in the organization's call-center division, which he was running, to suggest they meet.

"I knew we could learn from each other," Storey recalls. "I'd long ago learned that by reaching out to people, collaborating and sharing best practices, leaders could more effectively drive the business forward together."

They hit it off and found they both had skills and connections that were valuable to each other. They met quarterly until, in the spring of 2009, he was promoted. Soon after, he called Storey to tell her his former job was open and urged her to apply for it. Storey, who'd spent decades in sales and operations, won the position, overseeing sales and operations support for all AT&T consumer call centers as well as self-service and online operations. Today, she recognizes what a turning point that opportunity presented and what a pivotal role sponsorship played in creating it.

But she hastens to point out that her sponsor didn't just hand her the opportunity, she had earned it. "I was seen as a top performer," Storey says. "I'd developed a reputation for giving my absolute best, being a voracious learner, consistently delivering results, and saying yes to tough assignments. Men in leadership positions offered me opportunities, because I'd proven I could roll up my sleeves and make things happen. I'd shown that I would do whatever I could to drive the business forward and earned the trust and respect of the people who counted on me."

That's what you, as a protégé, must do to win and keep sponsors in your corner so that they'll pass golden opportunities to you. As Storey indicates, you must come through on two obvious fronts—performance and loyalty—simultaneously. Here's how she did it.

Performance

Storey demonstrated her stellar performance and commitment by:

- Delivering outstanding bottom-line results

- Hitting targets and deadlines

- Displaying an impressive work ethic and availability

At her first job, a printing company that published telephone directories, Storey spent the first six months making coffee ("I didn't even drink it"), making copies, and making an impression on the senior manager who oversaw all the firm's client relationships, including BellSouth, the firm's bread-and-butter account. He got her promoted to customer service representative and, six months later, put her in charge of the other representatives. "I clearly telegraphed to him, 'I understand the value of relationships and want to have a broader impact on the business . . . I am ready for more responsibilities,'" Storey laughs. More importantly, she solved his biggest business challenge. There was a chronic problem at the company: work orders were often late because of errors that demanded costly reprints. Storey put processes in place to improve accuracy, reducing both costs and delivery times—a win-win for the firm and its customers. BellSouth eventually acquired the printing firm, and Storey continued to rise to positions of increasing responsibility within BellSouth.

As she progressed, the deliverables changed: what her sponsors were looking for now was her ability to get others to deliver. The head of network operations asked Storey to help him build BellSouth's broadband capabilities. As she explains it, "He knew I could get strong personalities in different functions to agree on a path forward. I had no technical background in the network organization but he saw that I had the leadership skills to inspire people to collaborate and achieve results." Eventually, her role in evolving BellSouth from a voice to an IP platform won her the job of merging the firm's organizational and operational structure with AT&T's. This experience, coupled with her leadership of the women's network and various advisory boards, got her appointed vice president of consumer sales for AT&T in 2007.

What never changed, however, was Storey's unflagging commitment to deliver. "I was just wired to make myself smarter, to reach out and work with others to achieve results," she says. "Through that process, I developed a vast network of people who knew what I was capable of. That visibility has helped put me where I am today."

Loyalty

Storey also proved her loyalty by:

- Demonstrating trustworthiness and discretion and having her sponsor's back

- Burnishing her sponsor's brand across the organization

- Growing her sponsor's legacy

Storey's first sponsor put her in charge of the printing firm's sales organization. "Here I was, a young woman, leading a group of men who'd been selling space in telephone directories for decades," she said. Yet the move made sense, she realized, given her a track record of improving processes and strengthening customer relationships.

"My sponsor genuinely saw my potential," she reflects, "but I think he also saw me carrying on his legacy. I was someone who recognized the value of relationships. I'd sought him out from the beginning as someone I could learn from: he could get almost anything done by the way he managed the relationships he'd developed both inside and outside the firm. He believed there was nothing more important than delivering an exceptional customer experience, and I shared that belief."

Top achievers like Storey have repeatedly won sponsorship because they've come through on not just the performance front but also the loyalty front, *irrespective of their affinity (or lack of it) with the leader.* What makes sponsorship appear to be a dirty game is the fact that among those who've practiced it for decades—those in the old boys' network—affinity has been the basis for that trust and loyalty. Powerful men advanced the careers of younger men who looked like them and acted and spoke as they did. What makes sponsorship a mutually beneficial alliance in today's workplace is just the opposite: trust is now earned, cultivated, and deepened in a number of ways that utterly trounce the salience of tribal similarities, making sponsorship a potent and enduring career lever for everybody, regardless of race, gender, background, or sexual orientation.

MELLODY HOBSON

"I've had several sponsors in my life, but the one who made the most difference was John W. Rogers, Jr., who founded Ariel Investments. He had such faith in me. When I was just twenty-four years old he introduced me to Jack Bogle, investment guru and CEO of Vanguard. He said straight out, 'Jack, I want you to meet Mellody because she is going to be president of this company one day.' He gave me so much concrete guidance. His view was, 'Instead of you guessing what I want from you, Mellody, I'm telling you what I want so that we can map this out and then you'll be ready when it's time to lead.'

"And I came through for him. At Ariel I was known as his 'grasshopper.' Whatever he needed me to do, I did it. His requests ran the gamut, from crunching numbers to meeting with clients. Even family stuff. He would come into the office and say, 'My daughter had this sleepover last weekend and I need to thank the parents. Would you take care of it, Mellody? No one writes a letter like you do.'

"I was fanatical. My day was completely tied to his: the sun rose and set by his schedule. What leader wouldn't want this? This was heaven for John. My running joke was that I wanted one of me!"

It all paid off. Hobson's rise at Ariel was meteoric. She first moved up to client service and marketing rep, then to vice president in charge of servicing the firm's institutional clients. In 2000, Rogers named Hobson president of Ariel Investments. She was thirty-one years old.

Mark McLane, who today is head of global diversity at Barclays PLC, tells a story that illustrates how sponsorship thrives when a protégé takes up the challenge of legacy and reputation—and ends up burnishing the brand of a leader and a company. McLane used to work for Whirlpool, where he started out in sales. When McLane showed up at a company barbecue with his male partner Carlos Lemus, the firm's COO Jeff Fettig saw the opportunity to lift up LGBT issues and invited McLane to join Whirlpool's diversity council, which he chaired. While on the council, McLane impressed Fettig with his appetite for involvement with

Whirlpool's nonprofit partners—in particular, the Boys & Girls Club of Benton Harbor. Supporting and growing this particular organization was Fettig's passion. Long a trustee of the club's regional board, he had developed a vision for its future that included putting it on a much stronger financial footing (it was in the red) and building a brand-new facility. Fettig understood that if he were able to bring this off it would enrich his own legacy and greatly enhance the reputation of Whirlpool within the Benton Harbor community. McLane got it. He saw quite clearly how important it was for Fettig to triumph in this mission. So he joined the board, ran successfully for president, and drove Fettig's agenda. In the short space of two years, McLane turned a $125,000 deficit into a $250,000 reserve and drove the club's membership to a historic high, paving the way for the construction of a new facility. In recognition of McLane's many contributions, including his remarkable commitment to Whirlpool's footprint in the community, Fettig promoted McLane when he became CEO in 2004, making him head of global diversity.

Another proven path to sponsorship, star protégés make clear, is showing you won't shirk criticism and, indeed, will positively welcome the bad news as well as the good and the difficult advice as well as the easy. McLane succeeded in his turnaround of the Boys & Girls Club not because he knew how to work miracles, he says, but because he asked Fettig for guidance, guidance that included firing key personnel in the club's leadership. Storey at AT&T similarly notes that what won her the allegiance of her many sponsors was her appetite for the brutal truth. "I'd always tell them, 'Shoot straight, you cannot hurt my feelings, because I want to learn and grow and do the best job that I can,'" she says.

Women in particular need to make a point of asking for unvarnished feedback, says Debora Spar, president of Barnard College, because most sponsors, as a result of the pervasive organizational tendency to handle women with kid gloves, won't give them the critique they need. "We're overly careful," she says, "to praise and encourage women and go out of our way not to upset them. It's like Lake Wobegon," she adds. "All the children are above average, everybody's worthy of a gold star. And this coddling hurts women," she explains, "because when they finally get out there in the real world and get that first review and it's not a 5.0, they fall apart."

Spar attributes her own success as a leader to being subjected to a ton of criticism in her twenties. "I was lucky: I was raised by wolves, starting out at Harvard Business School," she says. "Men took an interest in my career, but they were harsh. I had to learn—early—to get comfortable with that." There were many teary moments, she recalls, during her stint as a research assistant for "a guy who was legendary for being both a phenomenal scholar and phenomenally tough." She worked for him for some five years, during which time they coauthored two books. "His highest compliment to me that entire time was 'not bad,'" Spar recalls. "That was the most laudatory thing he ever said to me. But that made me realize I didn't need to be patted on the head to work hard and excel. That was a great lesson to learn at twenty-one."

As a result of that formative experience, Spar readily distinguished herself among her peers by seeking out rather than avoiding criticism from her superiors. Leaders found it easy not only to level with her, she says, but also to rely on her to handle their highest-profile assignments. "They'd say, 'Give it to Debora, she's the only one with guts,'" Spar recalls. In her view, a capacity to handle withering criticism, stark reversals, and wretched news demonstrates—and this is the point—that you can be trusted to confront rather than shirk the tough stuff. This is the ultimate test of a leader.

This does not suggest that winning a sponsor's trust requires becoming his or her toady. On the contrary, persuading your sponsor that you can ultimately be entrusted with his or her job depends on demonstrating you will stand up to him or her and push back when necessary. Tiger Tyagarajan, CEO of Genpact, the India-headquartered business solutions company, attributes his success to the bond he cultivated with Pramod Bhasin, his boss and sponsor for seventeen years. Their bond was founded on the values they shared (both admired Jack Welch) and, interestingly, on their profoundly different leadership styles. Tyagarajan's primary job as COO, as he saw it, was to build teams from scratch by identifying and developing raw talent. Bhasin, in contrast, was inclined to pass on people who couldn't figure out how to evolve on their own.

So on numerous occasions, Tyagarajan relates, the two were at odds as to how to handle underperforming personnel. In many instances, Tiger pushed back—but he did this in private and not in public. "I'd go to talk to him after the meeting," he explains. "I'd say, 'Here's my thinking on this,' and show him that I understood his logic but also show him why it wouldn't work. And he was amenable to that input, as long as I kept it private." By sticking to his guns, Tyagarajan helped Bhasin transform Genpact from GE Capital's outsourcing outpost in India to a multinational info-tech giant. When Bhasin anointed Tyagarajan CEO in 2011, he stepped down completely—highly unusual for a departing CEO, who usually remains on the board—in order to give Tyagarajan complete latitude in exercising his brand of leadership. He trusted that it would work.

"It was a tremendous show of confidence and trust," says Tyagarajan. "We had very different styles. But in the end, I think he came to respect the very thing that distinguished my leadership style from his."

Nail the Tactics

- Hit the numbers. Meet all deadlines. Exceed expectations. Nothing makes you easier to sponsor than outstanding results, according to 62 percent of our survey respondents.

- Be able to recite—and make sure your boss can cite—
  your accomplishments in terms of what your firm values.
  It may be the scale of projects you're overseeing. It
  could be the number of clients you've won or retained.
  But know how you stack up against your peers and
  your competitors. A partner at Booz & Company told
  me how, when she was up for promotion to the senior
  ranks of the partnership, she armed her sponsor with
  the evidence he needed to convince others she was
  the best candidate. She reviewed all of her accounts,
  crunched the numbers, and compiled an extraordinary
  document detailing the revenues she'd driven. In
  particular, she demonstrated how she had contributed
  more to the bottom line than any other candidate.
  Her effort made it easier for her boss to push for her
  promotion, as he hadn't really known the extent of her
  impact. She's now a senior vice president.

- Get the word out on your successes. Since it can be
  difficult to brag about yourself, work with peers to
  sing each other's praises. A vice president at Merrill
  Lynch describes how she and three other women, all
  up-and-coming leaders but in different divisions of
  the firm, met monthly for lunch to update each other
  on their projects and accomplishments. The idea was
  to be ready to talk positively about each other, should
  an occasion arise. As this vice president explained it,

"If my boss were to complain about some problem or challenge he's struggling to solve, I would say, 'You should talk to Lisa in global equities, because she's had a lot of experience with that.' It turned out to be a really effective tactic, because we could be quite compelling about each other's accomplishments." In short order, all four women won promotions.

8

Develop and Deploy Your Currency

At forty-eight, with twenty-two thousand people reporting to her, Maggie finally wields considerable power as an executive at a global financial advisory firm. Yet only recently, she says, has she become a leader in her own right. Her boss, a West Point graduate, has worked with her to break a pattern she's repeated her entire career: what she calls "permanent lieutenant syndrome."

"I've always given 110 percent," she says. "Whomever I worked for, I gave my all, every day, ten hours a day, weekends and holidays—whatever it took to over-deliver. That endeared me to a lot of powerful men." She kept rising in the organization as a result, but always, she observes, as someone's trusted Number Two. Now that she's working on emerging from permanent lieutenancy, however, she's contemplating a new challenge: how might she stand out? What is her distinct "value add," her unique contribution? What currency does she bring to the table that might justify her status as a Number One?

The Power of Difference

In CTI's data set, permanent lieutenancy turns out to be frighteningly typical because, like Maggie, many women and people of color haven't figured out their special currency. They go the extra mile, and they're unquestionably loyal to their superiors. But they toil in relative obscurity, giving up their weekends not to elevate their own profile but rather to help their boss secure a fabulous year-end bonus.

Unless you have decades to spare, you'll need a different strategy. You'll need to differentiate yourself, not to *win* sponsorship, necessarily, but absolutely to leverage it to your own ends. You'll need to identify, develop, and deploy a personal brand. Or you'll wind up fulfilling your sponsor's ambitions instead of your own.

Dana, a vice president at a public relations agency, toiled for years in the PR world, first as a recruiter and then as an HR manager at a small executive search firm that focused exclusively on the PR sector. This experience gave her a unique insight into the industry: she understood not only the culture of the various firms but also the competitive tensions between them. "This was my currency when I came to this agency," she explains. "I had the inside scoop on hundreds of competitor firms, which allowed me to give this firm a sense of how it was perceived in the marketplace—a perspective that, as a privately owned company, it just didn't have. It was very helpful to them to have me tell them, 'This is your key differentiator.'" Over the course of three years Dana used this currency to differentiate herself, winning a sponsor and ultimately her promotion to vice president.

To home in on your brand or distinctive value, revisit your performance reviews, if you have them, or the self-assessment you conducted in chapter 3, and look at where you consistently excel. Better yet, ask your mentor for his or her insights on your distinct value add, or consult with your personal board of directors. Solicit the feedback of friends and family: they may be able to reveal to you the basis on which to build your brand.

Rest assured, you absolutely have an important piece of value to leverage. You just may not be projecting it. Ask yourself or others:

- How am I *innately* different from my peers?

- What about my background, experience, or schooling makes me unique?

- What skill sets do I have that set me apart?

- How does my perspective differ from that of others? What informs my perspective that doesn't inform theirs?

- What approach do I bring to solving thorny problems? How might this approach distinguish me from my peers?

Figuring out what constitutes the deepest well of your identity might help. Some people derive an enduring and reliable identity based on the school they attended. Others define themselves by the religion or culture in which they were raised. Still others see themselves through the lens of the expertise they've come to wield. If you think of people with globally recognized identities, people like Mark Zuckerberg or Coco Chanel or, on a more modest level, a leader on your team, it's clear that doing one thing particularly well can earn you that next rung on the ladder. What accomplishment might you reference or continue to draw on for distinction? Consider, finally, that what brands you as an *outsider* to the flock—even painfully so—might constitute your most distinctive edge, your most valuable currency.

Todd Sears is a successful entrepreneur, the founder of Coda Leadership, a strategic advising firm that focuses on diversity, leadership, and social impact. He is also openly gay. Early in his career, working on Wall Street, Todd hid his sexual orientation because he perceived it to be a liability—despite the fact that he'd come out in college. But in 2002, working as a senior financial adviser at Merrill Lynch, he realized he had the inside track to a community of affluent investors that the competition didn't understand: lesbian, gay, bisexual, and transgender (LGBT) individuals. This community certainly needed advice. Those with domestic partners faced thorny tax issues on both the federal and state levels, including titling questions and gifting problems. Sears, whose personal as well as professional experience had given him a working knowledge of these issues, knew he could guide them.

The trick was to make Merrill Lynch a trusted brand in LGBT circles. So, drawing on his familiarity with the target audience, Sears conceived of a way to bridge the gap. The gay community, he knew, was a major supporter of arts organizations such as New York's Museum of Modern Art and Lincoln Center for the Performing Arts—entities that Merrill Lynch also funded. Sears crafted an engagement model that leveraged these relationships, offering donor-appreciation events mixed in with financial planning seminars to well-heeled gay individuals in his network.

The New York seminars gave Sears access to an affluent and differentiated market. But he didn't stop there. Sears took his domestic partner program on the road, eventually delivering over four hundred financial planning seminars nationwide. In two years, his core team grew to comprise ten financial advisers in six cities. Internally, the team educated over 250 other Merrill Lynch financial advisers to serve LGBT clients worldwide. By 2007, Sears and his team had built the first LGBT-focused business in private banking and had attracted over $1 billion in assets to Merrill Lynch while also garnering global visibility by winning both the Human Rights Campaign Corporate Equality Award and the PFLAG Corporate Leadership Award.

Looking back Sears understands that what distinguished him from other top performers in his industry and won him the backing of powerful sponsors was the very aspect of his identity that he had tried episodically to suppress—his sexual orientation. "My being gay definitely helped forge the relationships that proved critical to my success," he says.

Nail the Tactics

- Identify the currency you already have and lift it up. If you're fluent in Spanish and your firm is expanding in Florida or Mexico, make sure your boss knows— and volunteer to help out on a project that needs your language ability. If you have great quant skills and your team is technically challenged, bring your expertise to the fore and make it useful.

- Acquire skills (currency) that your current job doesn't actually require, but that set you apart from your colleagues. An executive at Freddie Mac describes how, as a thirty-year-old working for a state housing authority, he spent hours of his own time learning how to underwrite mortgages. "It wasn't my job, but I wanted to know how it worked, the nuts and bolts. I spent hours going through this material with a yellow pad and a calculator until it became second nature to me. And now? I can be in any conversation about the financing of houses and be one of the strongest contributors."

- Reverse-mentor. Bring to your sponsor the skill sets or know-how she lacks. This might be technical or social-media savvy. One twenty-four-year-old sales rep, noting that her sponsor "wasn't exactly current in terms of the Internet," briefed her on job candidates whose résumés bristled with technical jargon and references to social media innovation that she simply couldn't comprehend, let alone assess for relevance. "I just helped educate her so she didn't come off as some kind of dinosaur," says the rep.

- Innovate. Access an underleveraged market, cultivate a new customer base, improve a process, or, in some other way create value. Rajashree Nambiar, head of branch banking for Standard Chartered Bank in India, saw a way to flex her cultural and gender smarts with the redesign of two bank branches in

Kolkota and New Delhi. As a professional Indian woman Nambiar had experienced more than her fair share of traditional male bankers, and had a hunch that women (who accounted for more than 50 percent of the clientele at these locations) would respond to a female-friendly environment. So when a market research firm confirmed her hunch, she pitched her novel idea to the executive committee: making over the two bank branches to be branches staffed exclusively by women, from the top financial advisers to the security guards. She got the go-ahead and proceeded to transform not just the "look" of the branches but the nature of the products and services provided. These all-women branches proved to be immensely successful, indeed one of them went on to become one of Standard Chartered's most profitable in the country, burnishing Nambiar's brand as well as that of her employer.

9

Lean In and Lead with a Yes

Julia was up for an endowed professorship at the university and, as she told it, the job interview had gone swimmingly. "The appointments committee was super-enthusiastic about my stature in the field and my contribution to the department," she said. "In fact, one member went out of his way to congratulate me on the big foundation grant I had just pulled in—the largest in five years."

But as the interview was winding down, the chairman of the committee peered over his glasses and threw her one last question. "If you got this appointment," he began, "you'd obviously have many more leadership responsibilities." There were nods all around the table. "And so we're wondering," he continued, "if we could still count on you to teach Economics 101?"

Everybody looked at Julia expectantly.

As she remembers it, she immediately sensed a test and answered very carefully, "Much as I'd love to continue teaching undergraduates, I think my focus should be on graduate students. That would align much better with my duties as lead person on the newly funded research." She flashed what she hoped was a gracious, accommodating smile.

Her response didn't seem to elicit any reaction. She shook hands with committee members and was politely shown the door.

She didn't get the job.

Shocked, hurt, and more than a bit confounded, Julia didn't see her error until a colleague and good friend who sat on the appointments committee called to give her some offline advice and feedback. As soon as he started to speak, she could hear the exasperation in his voice. He liked and respected Julia and was irritated that she had shot herself in the foot. "Never," he began, sucking in his breath, "never ever say no to that kind of question. What the committee was testing was your loyalty to the university. They know you're a star. You didn't have to convince them on that score. They understand you have a huge external reputation. What they didn't know and wanted to find out is whether you're committed to this institution. Econ 101 is not at the top of your list, but it is at the top of theirs. It's a cash cow for the university, one that can pull in 125 students a year if it's taught by someone with your star power. If you don't teach it, it will hurt their bottom line."

Julia tried to reiterate the logic that lay behind her response. But her colleague cut her short. "Next time," he urged, "just say yes. You can save the caveats for when you've gotten the job."

Attitude Is Everything

It bears repeating: just say yes. Hold back on sharing your reservations until you're in a position to negotiate.

Too often, CTI research shows, women don't. They lead with a long explanation of why they're not, regrettably, going to be able to step up to the plate. They're not able to fully commit, they explain, or they're not ready or perfectly qualified, or they have child-care issues. Women don't consider themselves capable of assuming greater responsibilities unless they're certain they have what it takes to deliver on expectations. They don't want to disappoint. They don't want to fail. They insist on being totally honest. So even as they come through on both essential fronts, and even as they distinguish themselves with a personal brand, they eliminate themselves from a sponsor's contention by indicating they're not willing to just go for it. To use Sheryl Sandberg's term, they don't lean in.[1]

Men, on the other hand, tend to overstate their abilities and their capacity to deliver. They also exude much more can-do energy than women. A 2005 University College London study compared men and women's estimation of their intelligence and corroborated earlier work showing that men of modest IQ award themselves higher estimated scores than women with high IQs.[2] In *Beyond the Boys' Club*, Suzanne Doyle-Morris demonstrates what she calls the female self-sabotage phenomenon in job interviews.[3] In *Women Don't Ask*, Linda Babcock and Sara Laschever see how women do themselves a disservice in negotiations by constantly low-balling what they could get.[4]

To be sure, women worldwide are more constrained than men. They're burdened by responsibilities on the home front as they continue to shoulder the bulk of the child care and the majority of the housework. Asian women in particular feel the weight of elder-care demands: 95 percent of Indian women and 95 percent of Chinese women working full-time say they have responsibilities to aging parents. Seventy-five percent of high-echelon women in the United Arab Emirates recognize how imperative international travel is to their careers, but 62 percent point out that cultural mores make it all but impossible to travel alone, and 71 percent contend that they cannot obtain visas.[5]

But constraints needn't be the first thing discussed when an opportunity is gleaming on the table. What's critical to communicate about yourself, as Julia learned the hard way, is not ability but eagerness to grab hold of the offer. Sponsors aren't looking for "yes men" in the political sense: they expect someone with real leadership potential to have real conflicts. When they throw a stretch assignment or a fear-inducing opportunity at you, they want to gauge your attitude, a critical component of the loyalty they value so highly, and not your ability, which they've already assessed. CTI research shows that 57 percent of sponsors value a can-do attitude in their protégés; 44 percent agreed that protégés should deliver 110 percent. Yet among protégés, only 32 percent say they "lead with a yes." A great many women, and at least some men, inadvertently dim their prospects for advancement or opportunity by failing to demonstrate their commitment first, their reservations later.

Say Yes Even If You Know It's a Qualified No

What does "leading with a yes" look like? The CFO of a *Fortune* 500 company gave us a great example. He wanted to put forward his protégé, Susan, for the newly vacant chief operating officer position. Her competence, credentials, and experience weren't at issue (she was the best qualified of the candidates), but he wanted to be sure, before risking his relationship capital on this candidate, that she had the "go-getterness" to outshine the other six contenders on the chief executive's short list for the COO position. So he called her into his office to explore her attitude.

"Susan, we've got an incredible opportunity opening up," he began. "It's going to require going to Omaha for six weeks, where we've just gotten the go-ahead to set up a new office.

We need someone first-rate, someone who can put together a crack team on short notice. You've got the know-how and the network, and you know what our priorities are going forward, so you're my first choice. What do you say?"

Susan didn't miss a beat. "Fantastic!" she said. "When do I leave?"

The next day, Susan returned to the CFO's office to reiterate her enthusiasm but also discuss logistics. She had a one-year-old, a roster of clients to maintain, and a major project she needed to wrap up. "I'm hugely fired up about the assignment," she began, "and delighted you chose me to carry it out, as I'm entirely confident I can get the job done in six weeks. *But*"—she drew a breath—"I wonder if I might propose a slightly different approach." Susan then laid out her plan: three days a week on-site in Omaha, two days a week overseeing the project from the home office. She'd send her own trusted lieutenant to Omaha to hold the fort and maintain momentum for the entire six-week period. Could that work out? She would absolutely lead the project, but this arrangement, she explained, would allow her to keep a close eye on the mission-critical work at the home office as well as the fledgling Omaha operation.

"Of course I agreed," this CFO commented. "I could hardly expect one of my top performers to drop everything and relocate to some outpost for a straight six weeks. She handled the whole thing like the executive I suspected she was, delegating what she could in order to lead what she must, all the while convincing me she was totally gung-ho." He added, "As far as I'm concerned, she's more than cleared the bar for the position."

Nail the Tactics

- Save "yes" for your sponsor. One biotech recruiter I interviewed observed, "Be selective about whom you say yes to: you can't say yes to everybody or you'll be spread too thin to ace any one assignment." Consider, too, how this particular yes, said to this particular person, will advance your career. It really comes down to being strategic about who you're cultivating as a sponsor.

- Propose solutions rather than present problems. You're perfectly entitled to accept a mission with caveats. But show enormous enthusiasm and gratitude, and don't throw your conditions back at your sponsor as issues you expect him or her to solve. Think through how you can make the opportunity work best for you. You owe it to yourself and your sponsor to give yourself the latitude you'll need to succeed. Lead with this solution when negotiating next steps.

PART THREE

Pitfalls and Trip Wires

You've homed in on your dream. You can see your destination, shimmering there on the horizon. And you've got in hand, finally, the road map that will get you there.

But I'd be remiss if I didn't warn you about the hazards ahead—the hairpin curves where you could veer off the road, the potholes that could swallow you whole. To negotiate these, you'll need more than driving tips and tactics. You'll need GPS.

In this section, I'm going to delve deep into three career pitfalls that other coaches won't poke with a ten-foot pole. The fact that no one talks about them is what keeps straight white men in power and the rest of us scratching at the door. First, for women, there's the ubiquitous and ever-threatening hazard of an illicit affair: sex with a superior or even the suspicion of it can take you out of the race. Then, if you're a person of color, there's the issue of distrust: if you allow racial divides to cut you off from potential sponsors, your fear of career-stunting bias will become a self-fulfilling prophecy. And for both women and minorities, there's the elusive but essential code of executive presence: fail to crack it and you'll lose your way altogether.

Awareness is your best defense.

To further gird you for the perils of this journey, I've harvested a slew of tips and tactics from professionals who've successfully completed it. Heed their wisdom, hold onto your road map, and I have every confidence you'll stay on track.

10

Sex

In 2010, a shake-up at the *New York Times Magazine* made headlines for what was an implied impropriety between its editor, Gerry Marzorati, and a young female editor he promoted from front-of-the-book to story editor, then to web editor, and in 2008, to his side as deputy editor. Megan Liberman, who'd come not from within the news group, as was customary, but from *Us*, the entertainment weekly, "became an extremely close confidante," the *New York Observer* reported. "The two of them were often seen together, and she was a close ally, staffers said." Staffers also said they found her abrasive—too outspoken, too outwardly power hungry. When a few longtime members of the *Times Magazine* team tendered their resignations, Marzorati, an editor once popular for his hands-off management style, came under fire for delegating too much power to his deputy. "Megan is a phenomenal, phenomenal editor," he told the *Observer*, explaining that the staffers' dislike was nothing more than professional jealousy. "I promoted a young woman, a really smart woman and an ambitious woman, and ambitious women make people uncomfortable."[1]

Were Marzorati and Liberman having an affair? Was her career rise attributable to sexual favors? Or was their relationship, as Marzorati maintains, a textbook example of how sponsorship should work?

Sponsorship is a necessarily close, even intimate relationship. Getting to know each other well enough to establish trust demands regular one-on-one encounters, possibly over the phone but more typically in person, sometimes at work but oftentimes outside of it.

Though these meetings may be strictly business, they can be—and indeed often are—misconstrued when they take place between a senior male and a subordinate female, because of the potential for a sexual relationship. While people's personal business needn't interfere with the business of work, an affair that involves unequals—between a powerful male boss and a junior woman, for example—tends to have an impact on the people around them. It unleashes, as the Marzorati-Liberman story illustrates, a treacherous dynamic that poisons morale, sows distrust, and stymies communication.

We don't know if Liberman was Marzorati's amour or protégé. We may never know. But you can see the problem: it doesn't matter what the truth is. Staffers *perceived* the Marzorati-Liberman liaison to be sexual. Some of the senior editors quit, so tainted was the well of trust and respect. With the gossip intense enough to prompt the *New York Observer* news feature, Marzorati tendered his resignation. Share prices dipped, as did morale. A mighty empire was shaken.

Sponsorship—already a rarity between men and women—suffered an enormous setback.

The Eight-Hundred-Pound Gorilla

Sex—the fact of it, the illusion of it—is the third rail for professional men and women. It can topple leaders (General David Petraeus is but one of a series of high-level casualties), destroy careers (Dominique Strauss-Kahn would agree), and torpedo the public's trust (often manifested in plunging share price: Hewlett-Packard stock took a 10 percent haircut when Mark Hurd was forced to step down in mid-2010 after he had an affair with a female subcontractor of HP[2]). The PR damage done by an illicit affair, given the media feeding frenzy that it inevitably unleashes, is so astronomical that firms waste no time in jettisoning their liabilities, however costly it will prove to replace them (as ESPN demonstrated when it fired both baseball analyst Steve Phillips and his twenty-two-year-old production assistant Brooke Hundley). Little wonder that most senior men (64 percent) are hesitant to have one-on-one contact with a potential protégé who happened to be a younger woman. There's just way too much downside.

This goes a long way toward explaining why men are so much more likely to sponsor other men, inadvertently perpetuating the old boys' club and keeping the boardroom barren of women. It also shows why women consider sponsorship to be a dirty game, one they'd rather not play. Perhaps if there were more women in power, up-and-coming females would seek them out as sponsors, thus skirting the whole third-rail hazard of a one-on-one relationship with the opposite sex. But because there aren't, up-and-coming women tend to conclude that sponsorship, sexually fraught as it might be, is something they don't actually *need*. More than three-quarters of the women we surveyed perceived promotions at their firm to be a function of hard work, long hours, and strong credentials. They're convinced that if they work maniacally hard to hit targets and meet deadlines, someone senior will eventually acknowledge their hard work and reward their sacrifice with a promotion.

But if nearly forty years of stalled-out female talent are any indication, this strategy simply doesn't work. Quite reasonably, senior management awards leadership positions to those who show initiative and actually demonstrate leadership, forging relationships with power brokers, seizing challenging assignments, rallying staff and resources, and driving team results for the firm. The worker bees who labor diligently at their PowerPoints and dutifully cross tasks off their to-do lists do not get to become queen bees. They stay in a support role because they spend all of their time proving they're good at support.

Men seem to intuitively grasp this. The vast majority (83 percent) we surveyed readily acknowledges that "who you know" counts for a lot. Fifty-seven percent perceive their own recent advancement to be a function of personal connections. It's not that they discount the need to be a producer: two-thirds acknowledge the enormous importance of credentials and track record. Rather, they perceive the value of relationship capital, utilizing it not just as a lever to leadership but also as a demonstration of leadership ability. Mobilizing other people to do your bidding—to help you win promotion or help you drive corporate profits—is precisely what leaders and would-be leaders *do*.

So men not only grasp the importance of strategic relationships with those in power, but also have no trouble cultivating or leveraging them to get ahead. Whereas women, leery of instrumental relationships and wary of alliances with the opposite sex that might be misconstrued, fall behind.

What can be done?

No Silver Bullet

Let's acknowledge that sexual tension in the workplace is a problem that's not going to go away—ever. So long as men and women are in proximity, sex lurks as a possibility. Indeed, with the world economy facing continued difficulties (flat-lined economies in Europe, an easing off of high-growth rates in Asia), men and women will be putting in even more hours away from home and family, making less time for an emotional life outside work and adding to the pressure to develop one at the office or on the road.

Let's also acknowledge that there are no easy fixes. I'm haunted by a story told to me by a senior leader at a blue-chip investment bank, a woman with a large team reporting to her. Midway into her career, newly a managing director, this executive became aware that her boss was holding regular meetings with the other managing directors (four men), at his home, over barbecued ribs and beer. "He invited them, but excluded me," she said, "and then they'd all lie to me at work about where they'd been that weekend." Months went by. Finally, she received an invitation and one summer Saturday joined the group at her boss's home. "Then I saw the dynamic at work," she explained. "Here I was, a youngish woman out on the pool deck with the guys, with my boss's wife hovering in the kitchen, peering out at us."

She could see how difficult it was for him to include her in any informal work gathering outside the office. But she fumed with frustration, because by excluding her, he signaled to the rest of the management team that she was not part of the inner circle. She knew full well, too, that the men had developed a special camaraderie by meeting like this, and that she had lost out on the trust built over months. "I understood his bad behavior was a function of his discomfort," she reflected. "But what may have felt like a minefield for him was a career killer for me."

Well, not quite a killer: this woman rose to a fairly senior position. But she feels her rate of progression suffered because she had no sponsors, and she had no sponsors because she could not figure out how to mitigate the third-rail risk for her male superiors. "There were men I reported to who wouldn't get into a cab with me, who wouldn't allow their admin to schedule them on the same flight," she recalled. "Looking back, I think this is what kept me always just outside the inner circle. I had a couple of near misses with sponsorship, but in the end, my bosses just couldn't afford to go there with me."

Corporate policies are no panacea for this, either. Even when companies have strict policies governing office romances or prohibit sexual relationships between managers and their subordinates, most people don't even know that these policies exist. As many as 64 percent of women surveyed and 65 percent of men said they weren't aware of any rules or sanctions around a consensual sexual relationship between a boss and a subordinate. And even if companies were to succeed in making clear the consequences for illicit affairs, that's not tantamount to preventing them.

But let's agree: we've got to make the workplace safe for sponsorship, because we all lose when someone with outstanding ability, whether as an innovator or a team builder, languishes or has to leave because of that third rail. Sponsorship is vital to fulfilling your potential, turbocharging your career progress, and delivering your dreams. And remember, during economic downturns and corporate restructurings, it's often the only thing between you and the door.

As an ambitious young woman, you cannot allow the threat of sex, scandal, or innuendo to keep you from cultivating sponsors, not in good times and especially not in bad. It's imperative you network, not just laterally but also vertically, not just with women but also with men. Having targeted an appropriate sponsor, it's then essential that you initiate and establish an alliance for the long haul, one that's founded on enough trust to enable you to ask for as well as provide the heavy lifting your aspirations demand. Cultivating a relationship that works to the professional benefit and not the reputational detriment of both parties isn't a question of *should*; it's a question of *how*. Specifically, *How can I initiate this relationship with someone of the opposite sex without invoking the specter of an illicit affair?*

How to Make Yourself a Safe Bet

DON'T HAVE AN ILLICIT AFFAIR WITH A SUPERIOR. To hear our interviewees tell it, everybody loses. You lose the job you have, the job you deserved, or the legacy you've built.

If you're female and the more junior party, our survey respondents confirm, you lose the most. Seventy percent of women surveyed say the junior female disproportionately bears the brunt of an affair, which is not surprising, but 53 percent of male respondents agree. That's because the woman endures a two-pronged punishment. First, when the affair is over her career trajectory changes, either because she requests a new position or one is forced upon her. Second, her reputation takes a dive from which it may never recover. "Men don't pass judgment on the guy," says Annalisa Jenkins, head of global drug development and medical for Merck Serono. "They'll say, 'Well, that's just who he is,' or, 'These things happen.' Whereas the woman is perceived as something of a prostitute or somehow lacking in social and moral values." That scarlet letter will not only make her an outcast at her firm, it will likely diminish the sponsorship she might expect from her network, dimming the possibility of her escape to another firm. "Her sponsors may not want to step forward and risk linking their reputation with hers," explains Kerrie Peraino, head of international HR for American Express.

RELENTLESSLY TELEGRAPH PROFESSIONALISM. Another critical pointer: do not send mixed messages. Flirting is a no-no. Sexually loaded jokes are off the table. Research CTI conducted on executive presence reveals that, for both men and women, making off-color jokes or comments is a top communication blunder (second only to making racially biased jokes or comments). For women, tight dresses, plunging necklines, short skirts, or barely buttoned blouses also send the wrong message. Seventy-three percent of leaders we surveyed cite provocative clothing as the number-one appearance blunder for a woman attempting to climb the career ladder. This is not to suggest, if you're female, that you suppress your femininity in the workplace. But it's imperative you be aware of what your clothing, makeup, hairstyle, body language, and communication style convey in the way of ulterior motives. Pat Fili-Krushel, chairman of NBCUniversal News Group, recalls having to take aside a new hire from Texas to spell out the style code in New York. "She was a great candidate, which is why I hired her, but her attire was inappropriate and gave the wrong impression," Fili-Krushel relates. "It can be awkward to give someone feedback on their style or appearance, but it is a part of an executive's total package, so I advised her she needed to adopt a more businesslike look"—or she was going to find herself in the corner office "for all the wrong reasons."

MEET YOUR SPONSOR IN PUBLIC. On-site meetings can work well; for example, bagels and coffee in the conference room or lunch in the cafeteria. Alternatively, choose a restaurant well-trafficked by office personnel, where you can take the opportunity to wave to people you know and make it clear you have nothing to hide. Dinner on a business trip may be unavoidable, but make sure the venue isn't the kind of place you'd ever go on a date, and don't order alcohol. Ideally, you want to routinize the time and place of your sponsor meetings, because regularity is what ensures nothing will appear irregular about you getting together with your sponsor one-on-one. An officer at Intel related how she chatted with her sponsor on the corporate shuttle, which ferried executives between sites twice a week. "It was the perfect opportunity to have a private chat, publicly," she says. It also won her her current position. "We would sit together on Monday and have conversations about the weekend, his kids, my kids. Then we'd start talking about what's going on at work this week, 'I have this meeting,' and so on. One Monday, I said, 'There's this job I'm thinking about.' He said, 'You can do that job.' He got off the shuttle and made a phone call. When I saw him on Friday, he said, 'You got that job, didn't you?'"

BE UP-FRONT ABOUT THE PERSONAL OR FAMILY COMMIT-MENTS YOU VALUE. Talk about your significant others—spouse, partner, fiancé, or ongoing relationship, as well as your kids, godchild, nieces and nephews, or adored pet. Make known the extent of your outside commitments—to church or temple, athletic league, community organization, yoga class, or poker group. Put photos on your desk or screensaver that assure others you have a network of emotional ties outside work. This doesn't mean inflicting your personal life on others. But you should give your sponsor the impression you're a person whose personal needs are met, who isn't overly vulnerable or available, and who's a safe bet to spend one-on-one time coaching or conferring with.

INTRODUCE YOUR SPOUSE OR SIGNIFICANT OTHER TO YOUR SPONSOR. Long before you're put in a position where your time with or proximity to a superior of the opposite sex might be misconstrued—a project demanding after-work and weekend work sessions, a series of out-of-town client meetings, or even that biweekly trip on the corporate shuttle—take advantage of social occasions to introduce your main squeeze to your sponsors or would-be sponsors (the Intel manager had met her sponsor's wife at a dinner by the time she and he were meeting on the shuttle). These occasions might be business functions—award dinners, community outreach events, weekend conferences—or they might be social gatherings, such as company-supported sports events or charity galas. By so doing, you'll telegraph the richness and coherence of your private life and tamp down any hint of an ulterior agenda.

BE CLEAR ABOUT WHAT YOU WANT AND WHERE YOU'RE GOING. This is especially relevant if you're a young woman working among senior men, according to a global leader at a large pharmaceutical company who referenced her own missteps as a promising young manager. Coming from a place of vulnerability, she observes, she committed the classic mistake of misconstruing signals from her male superior and inadvertently fanning the flames of a spark she should have snuffed out. "He was a bright, charismatic type with a big personality," she recalls, "accustomed to working long hours with a bunch of us high-achieving, ambitious young women. We connected on a professional level, but then, because he liked taking control, and because some of us weren't getting our emotional needs met outside of work, the energy changed." Alarm bells should have gone off, she adds, "but I was confused, because the attention this guy showed me felt like reinforcement of my good work—like a gold star." She managed to disentangle herself without major damage, but it taught her a lesson. She's now doubly committed to helping young women benefit from her hard-won wisdom. "Start from a position of strength," this executive suggests. "Know your professional goals and what you need to do to achieve them. Once I was secure in that view of myself, I was never in a position of vulnerability again."

Triage

You can make yourself a safe bet and still find yourself bumping up against the third rail. Your peers or subordinates may still perceive you as having something more than a professional relationship with your superior. They may shun you for simply receiving more than your fair share of the boss's attention. Or you might be exiled by leaders who cannot afford to be tainted by the suspicion that you're special to them. In these situations, your best response may be to confront your detractors head on.

WHEN THE GOSSIP MONGERS IDENTIFY YOU AS A LEADER'S FAVORITE, PROVE YOU WARRANT SINGLING OUT. It's tough being on a team when one person is consistently favored. It's even tougher if you're the person singled out, and you're one of the few women. If you find yourself tapped for the really plum assignments, pulled into meetings where you're the most junior person, or consistently chosen over your worthy peers, make the most of your opportunities. Come prepared to wow everyone with your contribution, work ethic, and devotion to the mission. Make known the kind of work you're putting in, the extra hours you're devoting, and the special skills you bring to warrant the consideration you're being shown. In a word, *own* your special status.

This may sound counterintuitive, but that's why it works: people who complain that you're receiving special attention or find ways to punish you for it are insinuating that you don't deserve it. If you behave as though you don't deserve it—if you're clearly embarrassed to be in the spotlight, or try to paper over the favoritism by acting surprised, or try to make it up to your peers by being super nice—you inadvertently reinforce their insinuation. Annalisa Jenkins of Merck Serono experienced this as a young physician in the British Navy. One of very few female officers onboard a ship at sea in a war zone, Jenkins couldn't help but attract the attention of her commanders. If there was a social event, she'd be asked to attend. If a general was coming onboard, she'd be assigned to the welcoming party. If a newspaper did an article, her face was the one photographed. "They called me 'the duty skirt,'" she recalls. "And there's no question, I was getting favored treatment." To compensate, she tried to be civil and gracious to everybody. "I thought if I were nice to everyone and worked really hard that would overcome suspicion of me using gender to avail myself of opportunities not open to others," she says. In hindsight, she realizes she might have fared better had she just exuded the confidence of someone who actually deserved the attention of powerful figures.

IF YOU'RE IN FREE FALL, PULL THE RIP CORD WHILE YOU STILL CAN. Sometimes the best thing you can do is acknowledge that nothing can be done—and leave. If you've been pinned with the scarlet letter and have done everything in your power to assert or prove your innocence and still can't shake the shroud of gossip, move on. Don't wait until your reputation is in tatters. Act while you still have good will to leverage. Carol, now a global media firm executive, imparts that advice, having endured, as a twenty-four-year-old, the Hester Prynne ordeal. She was an analyst at a Swiss investment bank, and her job entailed client service. With one client, a married man in his mid-fifties, she struck up a tennis friendship, playing a few Saturdays at his racquet club. On one of these occasions, he showed her some documentation he wanted to change. He was positioning his firm for an initial public offering and wanted Carol's input. Carol not only helped him with the documents, she persuaded him to let her bank handle the offering. "My math and accounting skills weren't as good as others at the time, but I was young and smart and a good listener," she explains. The IPO turned out to be the biggest piece of business the bank brokered that entire year, an outcome that should have translated into a massive promotion for Carol. But no sooner had she landed the account than her boss, accusing her of having a sexual affair with the client, took her off the account. "The whole idea of a young woman winning a big piece of business made him uncomfortable—and suspicious. He just couldn't believe I'd built a business relationship," Carol remarks.

Not everyone in management drew her boss's conclusion. The bank's CEO insisted she join the road show for the IPO, a vote of confidence she appreciated. Still, for the duration of the road show, she made a point of abstaining from all after-hours socializing, to the consternation of the client. "I did not dress provocatively, I didn't go out at night with the client or my colleagues," she recalls. "I did not want to be perceived as needing to do anything inappropriate to win my deals."

Once the deal was done, however, Carol quit the firm. "I really had no choice," she reflects. "There was little I could do to change their perceptions. In retrospect, I'm glad I acted when I did, before I lost credibility—and my self-esteem."

11

Distrust

Ron, an accountant with more than fifteen years' experience, felt he'd finally gotten his career break when he was rotated into the New York headquarters of his global financial consulting firm. An energetic man who prided himself on his strategic approach to high-profile cases, Ron was excited to join the team and fired up to deliver all he could for the executive who'd brought him to headquarters.

In the two years since that move, however, Ron has lost traction and momentum, largely because his sponsor left for another division. He's worked on just three projects, none of them client-facing. "The partners are not familiar with me and with my work quality," says Ron. "They're not about to take a chance on someone they don't know." He shakes his head, careful to control his words. "I'm certainly feeling excluded and not looped into things."

Ron feels invisible, and yet the way in which he undeniably stands out—he's African American, from the Deep South, with strong ties to his church—he's loath to leverage. He doesn't want any of his differences to be cause for distinction. He feels his track record and his professional experience (he has twice as much as some members of his team) should set him apart. Still, the longer he labors in the shadows, the less certain he is of what he brings to the table. "It becomes a lot of work to try and maintain confidence," he says.

Ron's story is disturbingly common among high-achieving minorities. Often the target of biased behaviors too subtle to call out or discuss, minority professionals feel compelled to play down their differences, yet are made invisible by their conformity. It's a catch-22 that suspends countless professionals of color in a no man's land, their potential recognized but unrealized, their aspirations acknowledged but unfulfilled.

An Elusive Solution

Sponsorship, as we've explored, could remedy this dire state of affairs. The sponsor effect on multicultural protégés is dramatic: minority professionals who have sponsors are *65 percent* more likely to feel satisfied with their rate of advancement. They are also far more engaged and committed.

People of color with sponsors are 57 percent less likely than their unsponsored peers to leave their current employer within a year. (See the sidebar, "Katherine Phillips.")

It's not hard to see why having someone in your corner who believes in you can make all the difference. Look at Ken Chenault, CEO of American Express. As a new hire at American Express, Chenault relates, "I was thinking as someone who was different from the majority of people in the company, 'I'll stay here for five years, get the experience, and move on to something else.'" But his boss, Lou Gerstner, made a point of reassuring him on this point. "You can go really far in this company," he told Chenault. "Here's what you need to work on."[1] Gerstner's sponsorship raised Chenault's aspirations, his visibility, and his credibility, since Gerstner was enormously well regarded as a leader and seen as a tough taskmaster.

An alarming 21 percent of Hispanics, 35 percent of African Americans, and 29 percent of Asians believe that a "person of color would never get a top position at my company" and most don't have a sponsor in their corner contradicting this view. Fully 37 percent of African Americans and Hispanics and 45 percent of Asians say they "need to compromise their authenticity" at work, a situation that breeds discomfort, stifles contribution, and distances them from would-be sponsors. The core issue, CTI research shows, is distrust: distrust of those in power (Caucasians, mostly) to reward them fairly; distrust of each other in the scramble for a few slots; and distrust of themselves to be fully competent and deserving professionals.

Discrimination and Distrust of Leaders

Chenault's conviction that no person of color would ever make it to the top at American Express proved to be wrong. But given what employees of color contend with in the way of hidden bias and even overt discrimination on the job, it's easy to see why so many share this view. Overall, 39 percent of African Americans, 13 percent of Asians, and 16 percent of Hispanics have experienced discrimination in the workplace owing to their ethnicity, compared to 5 percent of Caucasian men and women.

Discrimination takes many forms. An executive editor at MSNBC who is African American noticed that when she first began attending the crucial editorial meetings that decide the day's news priorities, her observations or suggestions were ignored and then usurped. "If I were to say, 'let's do X,' the room would just continue in its discussion," she recalls. "But then that idea would in a while find its way out of someone else's mouth, and then everyone would hear it, follow it, and understand it." CTI found that 24 percent of African Americans say that others take credit or are given credit for their contributions. Nearly a fifth (18 percent) of Hispanic professionals say that colleagues "have no idea" of their credentials. Eleven percent of African Americans say they've been mistaken for someone's assistant, and a similar proportion (11 percent) of Asians have been taken for someone else of their same racial background.

Compounding this, Caucasians often don't see discrimination, even when it's pointed out to them. At Lloyds, a manager of Persian descent recalls how, when she described to her white male boss her efforts to improve race relations at the firm, he replied, "That's great, but I am not sure that there's really a problem here." When she insisted there was, he retorted angrily, "You think that just because we have a white male in charge that this department discriminates?"

Because pointing out discrimination in a culture intent on denying it holds special penalties, half of all African Americans we surveyed and more than a third (36 percent) of Asians and Hispanics agreed that, if they were to reveal any struggle with bias or discrimination, it would be held against them. Professionals of color perceive it's best to just put up and shut up, further stoking the flames of resentment and distrust—and further distancing themselves from the sponsorship that could overcome the penalties they describe.

Distrust of Each Other as Risky Bets

You might think professionals of color would turn to leaders of color for the support and validation they need to fulfill their potential in the organization. Who better to give you a hand up than someone who's stood in your shoes and overcome the challenges you face? Who better to make you feel included than someone who knows how it feels to be an outsider? In fact, at the senior level, an impressive 41 percent of African Americans and a fifth of Asians and 18 percent of Hispanics say they feel obligated to sponsor employees of their same gender or ethnicity. "I'm going to look out for them as someone else won't, because I understand what they're up against," an African American exec at Intel told us. "That's where I see my leadership responsibility."

But many would-be sponsors of color, CTI found, hesitate or outright avoid allying themselves with minority up-and-comers. Those up-and-comers likewise avoid targeting leaders of color when they look for sponsorship. Both perceive the other as a risky bet, someone likelier to sink their ship than sail it.

Abdul, a manager at a financial services firm who is Nigerian American, illustrates why. He was just a year into his role when a junior black woman asked him to sponsor her. As the highest-ranking person of color in his office, Abdul knew that others of color would seek his advocacy. But because he was under such intense scrutiny, he felt he could not afford to make mistakes. This woman, in his view, was not "ideal." Four years into her tenure with the company and newly returned from a maternity leave, she had been passed over for promotion twice and had a reputation for being "very, very vocal." Abdul worried that, given her track record, he might be put in a position where he couldn't vouch for her. He especially feared that senior leaders might see his sponsorship of her as favoritism. "I will have to go to bat for this individual," he said. "Will it be seen as helping her just because of her skin color?" In the end, he decided his own tenure was too tenuous to take her on as his protégé.

Protégés of color, however, are just as averse to reach out to multicultural managers for sponsorship. They're far more likely—*143 percent!*—than their Caucasian peers to think that there are disadvantages to allying oneself to a high-ranking person of color. They see the benefits of an affinity-based relationship, but they don't believe a minority leader has the kind of traction a white leader does. An African American analyst with GE Capital says she turns to leaders of color for advice and mentoring. But for sponsorship, she's hoping to win over white men. "In finance, that's where the power is," she explains.

Distrust is a self-fulfilling prophecy: minority profession-als who distrust those in power effectively deny themselves the support they need to realize their leadership potential, further reinforcing their conviction that leadership at their company isn't interested in people of color. This, of course, goes a long way toward keeping the top of the house homo-geneous. Worn down by exclusion, buffeted by incidents of subtle bias, the unsponsored disengage, which fuels the stereotype that minorities just don't have the ambition or the wherewithal to assume leadership positions.

KATHERINE PHILLIPS

Academic powerhouses often labor in relative obscurity, conducting research, publishing their findings in academic journals, and burnishing the brand of the institution where they teach. But Katherine Phillips, the Paul Calello Professor of Leadership and Ethics at Columbia Business School, has made a name for herself as well as her institution. An expert on the value of diversity in work teams, she has counseled with diversity leaders at Goldman Sachs, Citigroup, and the US Office of Personnel Management and won numerous awards for her insights into leadership development and team management. With more than thirty articles in the mainstream press (e.g., the *Chicago Tribune* and the *Globe and Mail*) as well as in academic journals, and appearances on Bloomberg News, Phillips has created a wide platform to disseminate her ideas beyond academia.

What does that feel like for an African American born into a blue-collar family in Illinois?

Secure, for starters. "I remember when I first got tenure thinking, 'So this means that I can't get fired? I can tell it like it is without fear?'" Phillips relates. "That still feels wonderful. I'm particularly grateful not to need to think about questions of authenticity and being genuine—all of that is kind of behind me. I feel very confident about being who I am and make it my business to reach out to empower other people to be who they are. There's no way we can truly have diversity if people aren't comfortable being who they are. I am very wary of situations where people just want a clone of themselves in brown."

Phillips is upfront, however, about fact that she's never shirked an opportunity to speak out honestly or champion another minority. At Northwestern's Kellogg School of Management, where she was an associate professor, she advocated for a young black woman under consideration for a faculty position whose work she felt was brilliant but whose pedigree and research focus weren't highly regarded at Kellogg. "I knew that if I didn't advocate for her with a strong voice, she wouldn't be selected," Phillips recalls. "It was potentially risky. I do remember thinking, 'What if she fails to work out?' But because I believed in her—and in my

(continued)

own instincts—I stuck my neck out. She got the job and did well, and people started to trust my judgment."

With tenure and job security has come not only an enhanced ability to be herself but also financial security—a freedom Phillips treasures. "Success for me means an absence of financial stress," she reflects. "I'm not super rich, but growing up in a lower middle-class family, I couldn't have even imagined making the amount of money I make now. It's wow. It's very satisfying. For me there are huge satisfactions in having the resources to underpin my children's lives—money to spend on their health and their education."

Ultimately this freedom prompted Phillips to leave Kellogg for Columbia, as she perceived New York to have more racial diversity than Evanston, Illinois. "There's diversity there," she observes, "but there's a huge correlation, too, between race, socioeconomic status, and location. People who are poor in that town are black and live in a different part of town. There are assumptions that come along with being part of that community. I decided I wanted more choice, more control over my children's outcomes."

In exercising that choice, Phillips feels the tugs and pull of being an African American woman in a position of socioeconomic privilege. "My relatives will say,

'Why are your children at private school, why can't they go to public school? You turned out just fine.' It's seen as almost a betrayal of where I came from. I'm sure that many African Americans who've achieved financial success have a lot of conversations with themselves about where to live and what environments to put their kids in," she says. "But to have these choices is itself an achievement," Phillips adds. "To have to solve for this kind of tension, between culture and opportunity, is a privilege. I take great satisfaction in having earned that for myself and my family—and in being able to extend these opportunities, through sponsorship, to others who deserve them."

Vaulting the Color Bar

Despite the forces arrayed against them, promising professionals of color can overcome distrust—distrust of white leaders, distrust of minority leaders, and distrust of each other—to win and keep the advocacy they merit. Here are some proven tactics:

MASTER THE SOCIAL BANTER. Establishing a personal connection can matter as much, if not more, than proving you're a top performer when you're trying to attract sponsors across a racial divide. Sponsors tend to trust people they know, after all, even over people whose credentials are more stellar. Yet it's hard to get to know someone if you're convinced you have little in common or you're concerned that sharing your personal life will only serve to stress how different you are. The solution, as Kalinda, a real-estate analyst, explains, is to be a knowledgeable and enthusiastic participant in the small talk that occurs in the conference room or at the water cooler in the five minutes before or after a meeting. She points to her own learning curve, when she was working at ESPN as a financial analyst. "One of best things ever to happen to me was managing the NFL budget," she says. "I didn't know a thing about American football when I got there, but I recognized I needed to if I was ever going to be considered one of the guys." Every day, she read *Sports Business Daily*. And every day, she had an opportunity to flex her newfound knowledge with her colleagues and superiors, most of them men who were football fanatics. The whole exercise, she says, upped her game because it emboldened her to initiate or jump into conversations with her superiors, who were invariably impressed by both her command of the subject and her enthusiasm for it. "The teams, the games, the analysts—I could talk about all of it with anyone," Kalinda says. "Even now, if I hear football being discussed, I insert myself in that conversation, because I have something to add. For the same reason, I picked up golf a couple years ago. I'm not good at it, but I can talk about it, and that opens a door with my managers."

PICK UP A SPORT OR JOIN A TEAM. You don't have to become a golfer, but learning how to play bridge, training for a marathon, or taking up yoga (whatever resonates with your company culture) can all be incredible connection builders. You don't have to be good; you just need to be willing to learn something and join in. Deb Elam, chief diversity officer at GE, tells how she prepared for the firm's annual top management meeting years ago when she was a newly promoted senior executive. The meeting was held at a resort where golf was one of the afternoon activities. Eager to make a good impression, she took lessons for several months and invested in a custom set of clubs. When the opportunity to select activities became available, she signed up to join a foursome the first afternoon and very nearly chickened out. In a field of 150 that day, she was the only African American female. But she went ahead with her plan and even managed to enjoy herself. That evening, when she entered the evening reception—"a sea of khaki slacks, blue oxford shirts, and navy blue blazers"—a couple of senior white men came over and introduced themselves. They had seen her out on the course earlier in the afternoon. "Golf was the icebreaker," Elam observes. "I realized it's about being willing to put yourself out there."

DRAW ON YOUR BACKGROUND TO DRIVE VALUE FOR THE BUSINESS. Sharda Cherwoo, an Ernst & Young partner, describes how she previously led a dual life: she wore a Western-style suit at the office but dressed in a sari at parties with her Indian friends; she led a high-performing team at work but at home she tended to and cooked for family and relatives visiting from India. She preferred avoiding cultural differences to calling attention to them. Her mind-set changed after she told a Caucasian colleague that Diwali—a very important Hindu festival—was approaching, and was later touched to receive a "Happy Diwali" note. "It happened because I shared," says Cherwoo. She continued sharing more about her personal life, cultural differences, and interests, with the unexpected result of receiving additional professional responsibilities that tapped into her experience and heritage. Over time this has ranged from recruiting Indian "boomerang" talent (employees who've left Ernst & Young but who wish to return) to landing meetings with Indian business leaders in the United States and key regulatory officials in India. "You have to be proactive and find the unique value you bring to the table," says Cherwoo. "There is incredible potential to advance your career in showing where and how you can be helpful leveraging your relationships."

PROPOSE A PROJECT THAT POSITIONS YOU AS A PROBLEM SOLVER OR INNOVATOR. Where you see a gap, fill it. A recruiter for a biotech firm noticed that other biotechs diversified their pipelines by providing scholarships to undergraduates of color who majored in the life sciences. Working with colleges and her own team, she launched the company's first-ever minority scholarship program. Over the course of eight years, it made available more than $800,000 to promising candidates and attracted a significant number of minority graduates to jobs at the firm.

DARE TO ASK FOR HELP. This same recruiter describes how, in trying to launch an ambitious initiative as a new hire, she recognized she simply didn't have the experience, network, or resources she needed to pull it off. She sought out the department head, walked him through the steps she had taken, and candidly admitted she was out of ideas. "I don't know how to get this program successfully launched without your guidance and insights," she told him. "I've tried everything, and nothing is working." His response shocked her. "In all truth, I wouldn't have done things any differently than you have," he assured her. Then he pledged to help her win the buy-in among his peers that she needed. "Maybe developing trust has to start with the protégé, rather than the sponsor," she observes. "For people of color, it may be about overcoming the fear of being judged for needing help. I made myself vulnerable because I was determined this program would succeed. I wasn't going to let it fail just because, as a young woman of color, I was afraid to show I needed help."

IF YOU ARE PASSED OVER, FIND OUT WHY. Don't assume race is at issue; don't assume anything. Antoinette, a black managing director in a financial services firm, remembers how shocked she was when her boss's boss informed her that he'd be looking to hire someone to replace the woman she reported to, who'd gone on maternity leave and wasn't coming back. "I couldn't understand why I wasn't being considered, since I'd been doing her job for three months," says Antoinette. The more she thought about it, the more outraged and wronged she felt. After a sleepless night, she marched into his office and shared her consternation. "Quite honestly," he told her, "it just didn't occur to me to consider you. But, of course, I should. I'm glad we talked."

Her outspokenness won her the job. Never again, she says, did she make the mistake of assuming too much. As a result, Antoinette has a high-level circle of supporters both inside and outside the firm, including the CEO. "He calls me to discuss everything from succession plans to his son's college applications," she says. "He knows I'm someone who will shoot straight, who will tell it like it is. And I know he's one of several people who take my success personally."

12

Executive Presence

She was losing control of the room.

Her R&D team was around the conference table, a group of some twenty research scientists and biomedical engineers drawn from two separate sectors of the firm. They'd spent months together, agreeing to disagree, thrashing out solutions to problems for which there was no proven approach because the whole venture was new. Now they'd reached an impasse, and Hui Zhong, who believed in leading by consensus, couldn't coax them past it. Worse, the senior team, including the global sector leader who'd hired her to lead the joint venture, was in attendance. "They all saw me having a not-so-good moment," she recalls. "I was trying to get everyone to agree, but it was futile."

When the meeting broke up, the sector leader asked her to come to his office. "You could have been more decisive in there," he said, cutting right to the chase. "It's not efficient, having rounds and rounds of discussion. There comes a point when you have to make a call in the face of strong objections from the team. Make your rationale clear and issue a decision. That's what leadership is."

"That was one tough discussion," Hui Zhong laughs, recollecting that her initial reaction was to feel like a total failure. But in hindsight, she sees that counsel from her sponsor as a defining moment in her career. "Now I step up and say, 'Okay, we're not going to talk about this anymore. Here's the decision I've come to, and here's why.' It could be the wrong decision. I've made those, every leader has. But at least you're making it. And *that*," she adds, "is what marks you as someone others will follow."

What Is Executive Presence?

President Obama has it. Jamie Dimon has it. Steve Jobs had it in spades. So did Margaret Thatcher.

No man or woman attains power or exerts influence without *it*—executive presence (EP), that aura of confidence and competence that convinces others that you deserve to be in charge.

But what is executive presence? Do you have it? If not, are you getting the feedback you need to acquire it?

CTI delved down into these questions in 2012, fielding a nationwide survey and conducting a ton of focus groups. We found that executive presence comprises three universal dimensions. Whether you work on Wall Street or in Silicon Valley, how you act (gravitas), how you speak (communication), and how you look (appearance) count for a lot in determining your leadership presence. These three pillars of EP do not stand independent of each other. For example, if your communication skills enable you to command a room, your gravitas or aura of authority grows exponentially. Conversely, if your presentation is rambling and your manner is diffident or timid, your gravitas suffers.

While all three pillars contribute to EP, they don't contribute equally. Gravitas provides the real heft, according to 67 percent of the 268 senior executives we surveyed, more salient than either communication (28 percent) or appearance (5 percent). To uncover this elusive quality we conducted focus groups and interviews with senior excecutives. Their six top picks are shown in figure 12-1.[1]

The most important of these, we discovered, is the first. "Grace under fire." This amounts to keeping your cool no matter how much heat you're subjected to. JPMorgan's CEO Jamie Dimon displayed considerable poise, for example, when Congress grilled him in June 2012 for failing to

·1

...cts of gravitas

According to senior leaders, top aspects of gravitas are:

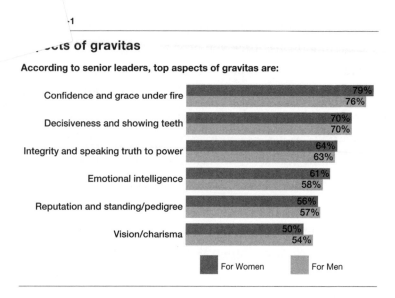

	For Women	For Men
Confidence and grace under fire	79%	76%
Decisiveness and showing teeth	70%	70%
Integrity and speaking truth to power	64%	63%
Emotional intelligence	61%	58%
Reputation and standing/pedigree	56%	57%
Vision/charisma	50%	54%

forestall some $5.8 billion in trading losses—a performance that won him investor confidence even as the losses in question drove down the stock. Exuding confidence is something any good actor can manage, but projecting credibility as well as confidence as you're riding out a crisis is truly the mark of a leader, our research confirms. (See the sidebar, "Sallie Krawcheck.")

Because your communication skills help project gravitas, they're the next most critical aspect of EP. But great speaking skills are not enough. You've got to be attuned to use them at just the right moment and know when to turn up the warmth and humor and when to unleash the pit bull. One executive (who is also a PhD) at a $20 billion food and

SALLIE KRAWCHECK

Be the best in the business. Stick to your guns. Show teeth. And no matter what, hang on to your integrity. These are the tenets that have defined Sallie Krawcheck's career—behaviors that have both won and lost her the top jobs at the biggest firms on Wall Street. But if she had to do it all over again, she says, she wouldn't change a thing. Success has always been on her terms.

First, there was failure. A miserable stint in investment banking and a divorce left her feeling "washed up at twenty-nine." But in 1994, with a new marriage and a new baby, Krawcheck found her career footing. She went to work as a research analyst at Sanford C. Bernstein, publishing hard-hitting and often critical reports about the health of Wall Street firms. Almost immediately, she made a name for herself. A mere twelve months after joining Bernstein and launching coverage of the Wall Street firms, she was ranked number one on *Institutional Investor*'s annual list of top analysts. The honor was unheard of for someone so young, so new to the business—and a woman. The following year, she was named number one again.

Suppressing self-doubt, Krawcheck stepped into her new power. "I liked the adrenaline rush" she says. "But

(*continued*)

more importantly, I loved making an impact. Because when you're number one in your category you can make stocks move and senior executives return your phone calls, your research is talked about in the market, and you're in the newspapers. That's pretty affirming!"

As director of research at Bernstein, then as CEO, Krawcheck took the firm out of the investment banking business, pushing it to deepen and grow its capabilities as an independent purveyor of sell-side research, even as her competitors were mixing research products with investment banking services. At the height of the 2004–2007 boom, this wasn't an obvious strategy to pursue, as all the easy money was on the investment side. Bernstein's earnings shrank, clients complained, and analysts quit to join the competition. But Krawcheck stuck to her guns because she believed that there was an urgent need for truly impartial advice—a vision that was spectacularly affirmed when the bubble burst. In 2002, when Eliot Spitzer went after the Wall Street firms where the conflict-of-interest problems were most egregious, Sanford C. Bernstein posted record revenues. Krawcheck made the cover of *Fortune* magazine, her image underscored by the caption, "In Search of the Last Honest Analyst."

"It was strange and thrilling all at the same time," Krawcheck muses. "I remember standing in the airport in Charleston looking at myself larger than life—a blow-up of the *Fortune* cover was on show outside the airport bookstore. It was quite surreal. But aside from the glamour of it all, I had this sense that I'd helped build something that really mattered. Bernstein was a firm that no one had really noticed, and now we were on the map. The story was almost biblical. So many people left the firm because they thought we had the wrong strategy, but for the team who'd seen it through ..." Krawcheck shakes her head, marveling at the recollection. "It was the pinnacle of my career, to have led that team," she says. "It was unbelievable."

Krawcheck emerged with an enviable brand: success with integrity. When Sandy Weill, CEO of Citigroup, badly needed to burnish the reputation of Smith Barney, recently tarnished by the scandals that had caught Citi in Spitzer's crosshairs, he called in Krawcheck—who was then thirty-seven, with an eight-year-old and a five-year-old—to run Citigroup's storied new acquisition, with its thirteen thousand brokers and analysts.

"It was really the big league," she recalls. "I'd go to the board meetings, and Sandy Weill, Bob Rubin, and Dick Parsons would be at the table—a group of legendary businessmen—looking to me to solve these problems. It was a watershed moment, to realize I had as much a voice in decision making as they did."

(*continued*)

Time recognized her accomplishment by putting her on its 2002 list of "Global Influentials." There were also some fabulous perks—a plane at her disposal, a chauffeured car, and the support and admiration of the thirty-five thousand employees affected by her dramatic reversal of Smith Barney's reputation. But the magical moment, the moment that symbolizes for Krawcheck the depths of what she had achieved, came some eighteen months later at a black-tie event at New York's iconic Waldorf Astoria Hotel.

"I walked in on my husband's arm, the flashbulbs are popping, and there's Sandy Weill, rushing over to greet me," she recalls. "At that very moment, my cell phone rings, and it's my son checking in for some input on his homework. I remember thinking, *isn't this fun!* Here I am at this ridiculously glamorous event, with Sandy Weill, my husband, and my son competing for my attention. What an amazing moment—'There's a legend walking towards me and I'm going to give *my son* the time instead!'"

Difficult times were to follow: when Krawcheck urged Citi's leaders, rather publicly, to partially compensate individual investors who'd sustained huge losses on products that Citi had sold to them as safe, her outspokenness cost her her job. Three years later, she would be ousted from Bank of America/Merrill Lynch, where her standout success in the wealth management division wasn't enough to counter a change of guard and political headwinds arrayed against her.

Through it all, however, Krawcheck has held on to her integrity, something her children discern and esteem if not always her employers. She recalls an incident where her family ran into Dick Fuld at a restaurant. Fuld was the former CEO of Lehman Brothers whose questionable practices precipitated the demise of his firm and kicked off the Great Recession. She introduced her son Johnathan to Fuld and, after they'd returned to their own table, started to explain to him who Fuld was. "Johnathan said, 'I know exactly who he is,' and started to talk angrily about how Dick should be in jail, not in a restaurant. I was surprised that he had such strong opinions and knew about Dick and became a little fearful as to what else he thought. I said, 'Johnathan, you know what I do, don't you?' He replied, 'Yes I do. I've read about you. You tried to give clients their money back. You're one of the good guys.'"

To this day, Krawcheck says, that moment gives her chills. "It was so important to me to have the approval of

(*continued*)

my son—especially since I had never self-consciously sought it. Learning that he was proud of what I had done on Wall Street—where so much is done that is not something to be proud of—that was huge for me."

Krawcheck sees nothing but opportunity as she contemplates her next stage and her next role. "I'm in a position now of choosing among a number of different paths, opportunities that are open because I've taken these risks and had these experiences." She considers this a moment and adds, with a grin, "I wouldn't trade spots with anyone."

facilities management firm describes how she used to deliver presentations steeped in data, models, and academic research, slowly building to her point—and quickly losing her audience. Now she presents the business case first, laced with key facts and short stories. She offers detailed data only when asked. "My strength today as a leader is my communication," she notes. "I've gotten good at reading my audience quickly and adjusting my style or tailoring my message accordingly."

While seen as far less important than gravitas and communication, appearance turns out to be absolutely essential to EP as a bar to hurdle first in order to be assessed in other, more substantive areas. Kalinda, the real-estate analyst, remembers her first meeting with the woman who would eventually sponsor her: "She told me, 'Go get your nails done. Wear some makeup. Figure out a hairstyle. You need a makeover, because you look like a little kid, and I am not going to trust a little kid to do a grownup's job.'" Kalinda, who prided herself on her grasp of intricate financial data and her preparedness, was taken aback. *This* was what she needed to do to break through to the next level? But she took her superior's advice and polished her look. Less than three months later, she was given a managerial role. "Part of it was timing," Kalinda says, "but definitely senior leaders' perception of me changed. They already knew I could handle more responsibility; it's just that now they *could see* I was ready for the next step."

Feedback Failure

Knowing what gives rise to executive presence (or destroys it) is half the challenge. The other half is in knowing how to apply the lessons to your role in your workplace. That's where a sponsor comes in. Sponsors, unlike mentors, will level with you, giving you unvarnished feedback on your executive presence because you're walking around with their brand on. The degree to which you're seen as having what it takes directly impinges on your sponsor's reputation as a leader.

But either because most women and people of color lack sponsors, or because their sponsors aren't living up to their duties, they're not getting this critical feedback. That was the disturbing finding of CTI's research.

A partner at one of the Big Four accounting firms told us about a young woman on his UK team whose appearance—she was curvy, blonde, and provocatively dressed—communicated something other than gravitas. Indeed, one client found her look so distracting that he asked that she be removed from the team. "It doesn't help to have the trolley-dolly image," the client admonished the team's leader. The leader, vexed at her and his own inability to confront her about her appearance, took her off the account. But he did ask someone in HR to enroll her in a course on presentation skills and client interaction. To her credit, the young woman made the connection between image and impact and transformed her look. "She's a different person now, a real rising star on the team," this partner commented. "I should have had the courage to give her feedback before."

This story shows not only how honest feedback can make a career-changing difference, but also how leaders struggle to impart this advice, particularly if the would-be Pygmalion leader is male and the object of his concern is female. Women are much more highly scrutinized for how they look and dress than their male peers but are 32 percent less likely, according to CTI research, to get any feedback from male superiors. Men, we've learned, will readily toss off correctives to guys they barely know—as in, "Your breath's a bit off; you might want to have a mint"—but will avoid confronting a female with much-needed guidance even if she's an important member of their team. There are reasons for this reluctance, of course. Male executives don't wish to make comments about a woman's appearance for fear those comments will be misconstrued as sexual harassment. It's wiser to ignore a hiked-up skirt than be sued for commenting on it. Yet senior females, our research shows, are no better than senior men at being forthcoming: only 39 percent of female survey respondents told us they'd ever gotten EP advice from a same-sex supervisor.

When women *do* get feedback, it's often distressingly contradictory, with criticism leveled from all sides. Unkempt nails detract from female EP, survey respondents told us. But they also found "overly done" nails to be unleader-like. Too much makeup undermines a woman's credibility, but respondents also faulted women for wearing too little or no makeup and looking like they're not trying. Being too assertive (and seen as a bitch) was problematic for women, but so was not being assertive enough (and being seen as a shrinking violet). The contradictions went on and on: being "too bossy" undermines a woman's EP, but so does being "too passive"; "tooting her own horn" detracts, but so does "self-deprecating" behavior. It's little wonder that 81 percent of women who do receive feedback tell us they have trouble finding the sweet spot. Staying on that knife edge between too little and too much seems to be extremely difficult.

A Stricter Code for People of Color

On the face of it, minority professionals fare better than women when it comes to getting EP feedback from their superiors. One senior executive who is of African descent recalled how, early in his career, a white sponsor told him his wardrobe needed to change—from the cut of his suits to the style of his shoes—going so far as to tell him where he needed to shop to correct it. "It was ear-burning, eye-opening stuff," he said. "But it fundamentally recalibrated the way I look and operate. You can't win membership in the tribe if you don't get that kind of feedback."

Yet this kind of feedback surfaces a deeper problem for professionals of color. Fifty-six percent of them feel they're held to a stricter standard than their white peers. So in order to conform, they feel they're obliged to suppress more of themselves or deny their own cultural dictates. "I look at CEOs of *Fortune* 500 companies and they all look the same—even the women," says Amita, a practice leader at Moody's who is of Pakistani origin. "They are all groomed to perfection. They have the same hairstyle and speak the same. You can fit them all into a box." Uma, a vice president at a major multinational, said she was criticized for her Indian accent. Unable to correct it, she has "de-ethnicized" her look. "I wear pearls and pearl earrings," she told me, explaining that Indians don't usually wear pearls because they're considered dead things. But compromising one's authenticity is what is required, she says, to be considered for any top job.

Men and women from East Asia are often told to assert themselves in meetings, even if it means interrupting the boss, a dictate that flies in the face of East Asian cultural norms, which emphasize deferring to those more senior in the room. But in Western corporate conference rooms, a passive or deferential communication style is seen as anathema to leadership. Ichiro, a former Cisco exec, recalls a promotion decision he had to make between two senior engineers, one Indian, one Vietnamese. He wound up choosing the Indian, even though the Vietnamese candidate was the better engineer, because in meetings with senior leadership the Indian pushed back, airing his opinion, identifying challenges, and noting where he anticipated needing help. The Vietnamese, in contrast, merely nodded assent when a leader tasked him with a problem. "You didn't get the sense that he was as firm on things, that if there were a problem he would raise his voice to bring it to your attention," Ichiro explains. "It's a requirement, at this level, to argue with senior executives. If you don't, you're not just perceived as ineffective, you cannot *be* effective. You have to have influencing skills."

Hispanic professionals also agonize about how to honor cultural gender norms while meeting corporate expectations. One Latina manager explains how she struggled to reconcile her upbringing, which had stressed being deferential to men, with her role at the firm, where she was expected to occasionally challenge her male boss. "I find this incredibly difficult," she says. She also ran afoul of the dress code: her waist-hugging, low-cut dresses were seen as too provocative in the

United States, she was told. "In Buenos Aires, a woman who doesn't flaunt her femininity will have a harder time getting promoted," she reflected.

African Americans struggle to overcome, as one black accountant phrased it, "historically embedded notions of being aggressive, angry people, people who will blow up." A large man, he described taking pains to alter his appearance so that he would come off as less intimidating, going so far as to wear glasses instead of contacts (which he preferred) and never rolling up his shirtsleeves. Another black executive described how, early in his career as a network television producer, he'd often come back to his desk to find a book or an article on "how to be a better black man"—for example, how to be a more involved father, a more supportive husband, a better team player at work—or essentially, as he put it, "how to be more white." While he knew it was well intentioned, it had a chilling effect. He stopped talking about his interests, background, and family, and kept to himself. But then his boss called him out for not being a team player. "You're too much on the fringes," said his manager. "People won't trust you. You've got to make an effort to join the tribe." In a clumsy attempt to be empathetic, he added, "I can tell you this because, as a Jew, I know what it's like to be black."

Attaining executive presence situates African American professionals in a classic double bind: if they conform, they're "Oreos"; if they don't, they may never win the trust or acceptance key to winning sponsorship. They're forced to constantly deal with the tension between fitting in and standing out, torn between adopting white norms of dress, speech, and behavior and honoring their own heritage and cultural norms. Some make a conscious choice, giving up parts of their identity in order to hasten their ascent at work. Others tentatively reveal aspects of their real life and hope their EP doesn't take a hit. One tax consultant described years of feeling "torn between two worlds," unable to reconcile his work self with his identity as a black man and a leader in his community. Only since becoming active in the black affinity group at work has he felt those worlds begin to merge. "It's a place to bring my passion, the same passion I bring to my church," he added. "The tension's still there, but I'm doing better."

Cracking the Code(s)

Given these hurdles, one might well ask, Is it possible, as a female or person of color, to crack this code? Is it worth it?

Make no mistake: however casual your office, however small your firm, however unorthodox your industry, to get the plum assignments, to be put on the best projects, to be given access to the inner circle where the real decisions are made, you've got to be *perceived* as leadership material. You've got to look, sound, and act the part. If you're serious about attaining your career goals, you have to seriously cultivate executive presence.

To be sure, this isn't easy. But CTI has amassed some pointers to help you hurdle this trip wire—guidance from those who've tested it in a variety of environments.

Appearance

- Look to up-and-coming leaders in your organization for clues on the unwritten rules for appearance. There is no one executive look; one size does not fit all. Every industry has its own code. Our survey data surfaced wide disparities in what employees at formal, hierarchical firms prized over what staffers at casual, flat organizations considered critical to EP. Those who work in finance, for instance, are 60 percent more likely to prioritize appearance than those who work in tech and engineering. Employees in hierarchical corporate environments are more than three times as likely as those in flat organizations to cite "polish" as a key contributor to a woman's EP. To crack the code at your office, take your cues from those in charge.

- No matter how casual your dress code, look pulled together. At ESPN, where staffers routinely attend sports events, the Friday dress code is "sideline casual," meaning that if you show up for work in ratty jeans and a T-shirt or sweater, no one will notice. But that's the point, says Kalinda, who in 2010, when she oversaw production budgets for the NFL, used to show up in jeans and a T-shirt: no one noticed her. She upgraded her Friday casual attire to tailored trouser jeans and a blazer and by late 2010 was given responsibility for ESPN 3D in addition to *Monday Night Football*. She's convinced that elevating her game on the appearance front was part of the reason why.

- Look appropriate in your environment, but authentic to yourself. Be true to your personality, style, and body type. A look that isn't you—that has everyone scratching their heads—can actually sap your executive presence. The trick, especially for women and professionals of color, is to find the overlap between being true to yourself and impressive in the workplace. Miniskirts or huge hoop earrings may be authentic to you, for example, but they're still inappropriate for most corporate environments. "What you wear should underline your gravitas, not throw it into question," says Kerrie Peraino, head of international HR for American Express.

- Win yourself a seat at the table; then dare to stand out. Paying extra attention to your appearance— your dress, grooming, posture, and bearing—at the very least ensures you don't get written off before your other attributes are considered. As one senior executive puts it, looking the part will get you into the room where your subtantive skills and talents can be fairly assessed. "The more familiar people are with you and your skills, the more bandwidth and leeway you have with different styles," she says. "But the less familiar people are with you, the narrower that bandwidth, and the more easily distracted they are by inappropriate dress and appearance." One of the decided benefits of moving up the ladder is that your leeway grows until, ironically, you can get away with just about anything in the way of personal expression, whether it's a Diane von Furstenberg wrap dress and Stuart Weitzman stilettos (think Diane Lockhart in CBS's *The Good Wife*), scruffy, ill-fitting suits (think Warren Buffet), or that plunging neckline with fitted bodice and full skirts (Oprah Winfrey). It may be lonely at the top, but at least you get to wear what you want.

Communication

- Tone it down. Women (or indeed men) don't need a deep bass voice to command attention, but if they're shrill, they'll definitely lose their audience. Attorney Kent Gardiner, chairman of the law firm Crowell & Moring LLP, has an interesting perspective on tone of voice. He tells of one client asking him to remove the female associate assigned to his case because of her abrasive, high-pitched tone. Lynn Utter, COO of Knoll, the furniture company, likewise mentions

this as a pitfall, noting that, oftentimes, it surfaces
for women when they are feeling offended, ignored,
or wronged. Her advice: remove emotion from the
equation, and you're less likely to be shrill.

- Overprepare. You'll feel more in control if you've
  spent more than enough time preparing, which will,
  in turn, keep your voice in the right register and hold
  the attention of your audience. "Being well prepared
  for a meeting leads to confidence, confidence allows
  you to command the room, and your command of the
  room earns followership," says Barbara Adachi, head
  of human capital at Deloitte.

- Less can be more. Jane Shaw, former chairman
  of Intel's board, affirms that you can't afford to be
  a wallflower at meetings. But she cautions against
  speaking up just to for the sake of it. "Inject a
  comment when you have something fresh to add. If
  you're asked for an update, stick to new items. Invite
  others to add their opinion rather than babble on. If
  someone has not weighed in, you might throw it to
  them when you finish," she advises.

- Get to the point. Linda Huber, Moody's chief financial
  officer, suggests that women, when they intervene
  in a discussion, pare back the preamble: "Don't start
  with, 'I've spent hours staying awake thinking about
  this and talked to thirty-seven people.' It's okay to

say, 'I have a different point of view' and then back
it up with two or three reasons you can support with
evidence and data."

- Invoke your vertical. Anne Erni, who today heads
up leadership, learning, and diversity at Bloomberg,
describes an incident early in her career on Wall
Street where her body language helped her pull off an
unpopular decision with a hostile crowd. "The other
executives were ganging up on me, literally yelling
and cursing. Meanwhile, forty people were waiting
for us to come forth with a decision. I had to focus on
getting to that goal. I sat there and, with every ounce
of energy, just kept pushing my feet into the floor,
sitting tall, and making my spine and head straight.
Then I leaned forward and spoke. It not only got me
through that awful moment, but I won their respect,
and we moved forward."

- Polish your small talk. On either side of formal
meetings what you have to say is huge. As we've
already explored, a key to building trust is sharing
personal details and "mastering the banter." Since the
best banter is not work related, but about sports or
current events, it's important that you be conversant in
these topics and attuned to the headlines of the day. It's
easier to leap at opportunities to establish commonality
if you've got plenty of fodder to draw on.

Gravitas

- When you know you're right, stick to your guns. Lynn Utter remembers the meeting that won her serious attention and the support of leaders. At a gathering of the board to discuss a joint venture, a discussion quickly devolved into squabbling. Utter spoke up. "Here's what we have to do," she announced, confident she was right because she'd done her homework. "Either we step up and invest or we call off the whole thing." That got their attention. Then she laid out her case. One of the board members told her later, "I had no idea who you were or what you were made of, but in that moment you showed you had what it takes."

- Show teeth. This doesn't mean you should act aggressively. Rather, you want to assure others that you mean business, that you can get things done. A managing director at a medical supply firm describes how she handled a potentially explosive situation when a payroll glitch stiffed some eight hundred employees out of their monthly paychecks. She had little time to act: the firm was in the midst of union negotiations, and if left uncorrected, the vendor mishap might well trigger a strike. She got on the phone with the local manager and his team to determine immediate next steps. "I'm committed to seeing this through with you," she assured them. Then, privately, she made it clear to that manager that both their reputations were at stake and she would hold him accountable for meeting the goals she'd laid out. "I knew that yelling and stamping my feet in public would not get me the cooperation I needed to resolve the crisis quickly," she says. "So I let my colleague know he was supported, but that his job was on the line. He heard me."

- Assert your integrity. Tim Melville-Ross, chairman of Royal London Mutual Insurance, describes a decision early in his tenure as CEO of Nationwide, the biggest mortgage lender in the UK, that nearly derailed his career. Under pressure to improve margins, he green-lighted a questionable, if common, banking practice on the advice of a new board member. The media called him on it, and he immediately made an apology. "You can afford to make a few mistakes, provided you acknowledge you erred, publicly—and provided you put them right," he says.

PUTTING IT ALL TOGETHER

I've made my own mistakes in cracking the executive presence code.

When I was in my late twenties, I joined the Barnard College faculty as assistant professor of economics. I reckoned it was OK to be young and fun because I was working on a college campus, not Wall Street. So I grew my hair to my waist and wore long, flowing, ethnic skirts. My favorite was handmade and had a rather loud patchwork quilt pattern. I didn't understand that looking as though I was on my way to Woodstock got in the way of establishing authority on the job. At twenty-eight, it was a stretch to convince anyone I was a professor and not another student. The last thing I needed was to compound the problem by dressing like one.

A few years later, I veered in the opposite direction. In a new job where my dealings were with a council of corporate CEOs and labor leaders (ninety-nine men and one woman), I decided I needed to look super-serious, so out went the flowing skirts and in came the gray suits. Small, slight, and brown-haired, I succeeded only in fading into the woodwork, a problem exacerbated by my communication style. One habit

(*continued*)

I had taken from academe was a preference for lengthy, nuanced arguments supported by a ton of compelling facts. But what had won me a "teacher of the year" award on campus did not go over well in the conference room. CEOs, I belatedly understood, have short attention spans and need terse, pithy feedback.

Not until I was well into my third career as an author and an advocate did I hit my stride. The tremendous media exposure that came with the publication of my first blockbuster book put me on a steep learning curve. There's nothing like watching a rerun of an unsuccessful appearance with Oprah or Charlie Rose to etch into your mind what's wrong with how you looked, what you said, and how you said it. I was forced to try out new approaches.

I learned to wear simple, jewel-toned dresses with closely fitting black jackets—or the reverse. I added into the mix a pair of fabulous high-heeled shoes or boots. Hair was shoulder-length and straight (no flips); makeup was subtle. Most important, I learned how to tell short, powerful stories. Sure, I continued to do a ton of research and produce compelling evidence for whatever position I was taking. But I learned that a narrative connects to hearts and minds in a way that a barrage of facts does not. It took me until age forty to put this together, and the journey was rocky.

What I couldn't have known at seventeen was that the right look was only the beginning. But what I might have known earlier—had someone given me the guidance—was how much executive presence would figure into success. Without it, I would not be perceived as a powerhouse, whatever my credentials and experience. Perhaps perception shouldn't count for so much. But to ignore the importance of looking and acting like a leader is to imperil your chances of becoming one.

Epilogue
Castles

Career success starts with building a castle—to give shape and form to a vision of where you want your journey to take you. The more splendid you can make this castle the better—it will deepen your resolve and spur you on. And believe me, you'll need all the inspiration you can muster. In today's intensely competitive work environment, with hordes of contenders grasping at the same trophy, you'll need fierce determination to win the race. As we know, you'll also need sponsors—two or three of them—to steer you onto the fast track and create the conditions that allow you to come in first.

Without sponsors, I wouldn't be where I am today. Sponsorship plucked me from a Welsh coal-mining town and put me on track at Cambridge. Sponsorship vaulted me from academia into public policy. Sponsorship, ultimately, delivered me to my destination. Today as the founding president of the Center for Talent Innovation and chair of the Task Force for Talent Innovation, I lead a private-sector consortium of some seventy-five global companies committed to changing the face of leadership around the world.

My recent and most magnificent castle that took shape in late 2003 over a five-hour lunch at the venerable Century Club in midtown Manhattan. We were a determined party of twenty gathered around the crystal- and silver-laden table that day: ten business leaders, four nonprofit directors, two scholars, two journalists, an Equal Employment Opportunity Commission head, and me. I had gathered this distinguished group, cashing in every chip I had, on the basis of what I knew to be our shared frustration: the unfulfilled promise of the civil rights and women's movements. The activism of the sixties and seventies had achieved an impressive measure of equal access to education and career opportunity, but forty years later, qualified women and people of color were clustered on the lower and middle rungs of career ladders and had yet to break through to the top tiers of management. The C-suite in corporate America remained, in 2003, stubbornly pale and male. Thwarted by hidden bias, or pulled off track to raise children or tend to aging parents, women and minorities were seriously stalled. This represented a brain drain the country could ill afford.

Lunch was cleared; platters of the club's signature macaroons were served. What was needed, we agreed, was a fresh wave of activism devoted to keeping women and minorities on track to leadership by addressing the pushes and pulls knocking them off. We agreed, too, on where this action needed to come from: the private sector. The public sector in the United States had steadily backed away from providing the policies or the pressure that might have leveled the playing field. We envisioned a task force comprising senior executives from the world's leading companies, allied with a newly formed research center. I would head up both entities.

The discussion deepened. We hammered out a multiyear agenda that would create pathways to power for women and other previously excluded groups, underpinned by a watertight business case. My economist training told me that this was key. Inclusive leadership won't happen if it's merely a nice thing to do. To become a top priority, it needs to speak urgently to the bottom line.

By mid-afternoon, we'd laid out a five-pronged program, which, by the way, proved to have remarkable staying power. These five elements formed a foundation for the task force's work that would ultimately culminate in nine *Harvard Business Review* articles and three research reports. Here's what we agreed to that day:

1. A project centered on women's progression, which tackled women's discontinuous careers and the struggle to win champions at the top of the house.

2. A project on the progression of people of color—African American, Asian, and Hispanic talent in the United States, but also multicultural, local talent in Brazil, Russia, India, and China.

3. A project on the differentiated values and aspirations of young people in the workforce.

4. A project on the retention and acceleration of LGBT professionals that zeroed in on the payoff to individuals and companies when employees feel they are able to own and disclose their sexual identities.

5. A project on the challenge of extreme jobs—how companies can build resilience, tame the demands of our 24/7 work culture and make careers sustainable for both women and men.

We decided to kick off with the first agenda item, the women's project. Not only was I exceptionally well prepared to spearhead this piece—I had recently published a book, *Creating a Life*, which explored how women might successfully integrate career and family—but the topic had just become hugely controversial.

Four days before my Century Club luncheon, the *New York Times Magazine* published "The Opt-Out Revolution." Lisa Belkin—then a contributing writer to the *New York Times*—had followed eight highly qualified women (Princeton grads) as they traded in their briefcases for babies and book clubs. Her underlying thesis: across America, professional women were quitting their jobs, abandoning promising careers to devote themselves to home and family. Her conclusion: the workplace was not rejecting qualified women; rather qualified women were rejecting the workplace.

Belkin's piece provoked a huge response. In chat rooms and in e-mails to the *New York Times* thousands of women shared their angst. I was particularly interested in the reaction of working women, many of whom disagreed with the article. Some talked poignantly about how they loved their work, how it gave meaning and purpose to their lives. Others talked about how they needed to work to support themselves and their families. In the words of one, "How can Belkin infer a mass exodus from the work/life choices of a handful of privileged women, all of whom happened to be married to wealthy men?" While sharing the general dismay at the elitism of the article, I mostly worried about the potential impact on employers. For business leaders reluctant to develop or promote women, this piece provided the perfect justification for inaction. It was time to introduce solid new research into the national conversation.

My lunch companions and I all agreed: a rigorous, data-driven study on the actual career paths of well-qualified women employed in a range of sectors across the economy should kick off my new think tank and task force. Our findings would derive from a robust national sampling (rather than eight Princeton grads) and would showcase solutions—on-ramping programs developed by task force companies eager to help women get back on track. Given the rich data I'd amassed for *Creating a Life*, I knew we'd be able to prove that there was no mass exodus. Women were not throwing in the towel. Sure there were issues and obstacles—many of which I intended to tackle—but women increasingly needed their earning power and sought to fulfill dreams beyond home and family.

The wood-paneled room glowed with energy and enthusiasm, but the light was fading. I knew I needed to make "the ask" now, before momentum waned and our grand vision succumbed to inertia. The castle we were building required tens of thousands of dollars in start-up funding. I urgently needed to convert support into buy-in and backing.

I straightened my back, squared my shoulders, and looked piercingly at the most powerful person in the room, whom I had seated opposite me. "We're coming up to 4 p.m. and it's crunch time," I said, my voice low, my tone deliberate. "We can change the conversation and create urgent action on these issues. This think tank and task force can change the face of leadership in this country. Each of you is uniquely positioned to rally resources. I will make a full-on commitment—signing over my life for the next several years—if you will each commit serious support. What I need right now is seed money—from you, your organization, or other heavy-hitters you can sign up for this cause."

When I walked out of the Century Club that afternoon, I had six pledges of financial support and the beginnings of a powerful board of directors.

I had asked, in essence, for sponsorship. I asked these movers and shakers to take a bet on me: to put their resources and their clout behind my vision and invest in my venture. They came through. The Hidden Brain Drain Task Force (later to be renamed the Task Force for Talent Innovation) officially launched in February 2004.

I didn't get sponsorship because I asked for it. No one gets it that way. I got it because I'd earned it. In early 2004, I was reaping the fruits of a harvest I'd sown over many years. I didn't have a seven-point plan (that awaited the writing of this book), but by learning from my early mistakes and becoming much more intentional, I'd put in place the most critical elements:

- I'd built a castle and embraced my dream.

- I'd learned how to exude EP.

- I'd targeted the right leaders—and gotten myself in front of them.

- I'd figured out that for every "get," I needed to give.

- I gave 110 percent and stood firm in my loyalties, thereby establishing a two-way street.

- I'd discovered my special currency—the value-added that was all my own but that would effectively burnish and expand on what others brought to the table.

- And I absolutely led with a yes. I learned to lean in with everything I had.

Embracing the Dream

It took a while, but I arrived at a vision and doggedly built my castle. After Barnard and the Economic Policy Council, I struggled to stay on the career track. Five children and a needy family in Wales meant that I took my share of off-ramps and on-ramps. But I did write some powerful books, demanding endeavors that truly honed a vision: *When the Bough Breaks*; *The War Against Parents*, which I wrote with Cornel West; and *Creating a Life* among others. I'd also testi-fied in Congress on behalf of parenting leave and helped Bill Clinton pass the landmark Family and Medical Leave Act. By the early 2000s, I was ready for the big push. As I recounted earlier in this chapter, I had become totally vested in the idea of founding a task force and research center that would propel women—and other previously excluded groups—into lead-ership. I was convinced that the world would be a better and more prosperous place if there were more diversity at the top.

Nailing Executive Presence

Gravitas wasn't an issue. A PhD in economics and ten years in academe meant I was able to convey intellectual horsepower. I'd also cracked the code on communication. A decade of grueling book tours had knocked me into shape. It wasn't a process I'd care to repeat. I made myself watch endless reruns of a particularly tepid, boring interview I'd done with Charlie Rose, forcing myself to see, through the winces, why I was so yawn-inducing. This painful exercise taught me how to be smart, pithy, and charming in thirty-second and three-minute sound bites.

Appearance was, curiously, the real challenge for me. It wasn't a question of being frumpy or overweight (again, those grueling book tours had trained me up and lifted my game). Rather, it was a question of age. When you're a woman of a certain age, how do you signal to the world that you have the spark, chutzpah, vigor, and vitality to kick off a hugely ambitious multiple-year project?

I've discovered that for a middle-aged female, nothing signals vitality more than toned arms with a discreet ripple of muscle. That's right: making a fabulous first impression boils down to biceps. And my upper arms are *fantastic* (not quite up to Michelle Obama's standard, but close). I'm a swimmer and relentless about it. However jammed my schedule, I get to a pool four times a week for my allotted laps. To save time, I've perfected the art of not getting my hair wet (blow-drying long hair can take an impressive forty minutes). I wear a

1950s-style swim cap with thick rubber guards and purple petals, which looks quite ridiculous. But who cares—I love my exercise regime. It soothes my soul and tones my body.

So these days my professional wardrobe centers on slim-cut dresses—high necked but bare armed. Sure, I often team these dresses with a well-cut jacket or a graceful scarf because the no-sleeve look is not always appropriate. But it's the rare business meeting that doesn't allow me to unsheathe those biceps and prove I'm up to the task before me.

Targeting the Right Leaders

When I began to identify potential backers for my castle, I knew I needed a mix: prominent figures from the policy or scholarly world, certainly, but also powerhouses from the private sector. I did, after all, need major funding. I'd learned my lesson from my Barnard days. This time around I wasn't seeking friendly but ineffectual mentors; instead I was targeting people who had the capability of backing me and my new venture.

I started with Carolyn Buck Luce, a senior partner at Ernst & Young. We'd met socially some three years previously (she was the wife of the minister at my church). Not only did we like one another enormously—we immediately clicked—but she was an ideal potential sponsor. Carolyn was a prominent private-sector woman, precisely the kind of leader I needed on my side. She shared my passion for women's progression and believed in my value and my worth.

Understanding the "Give" as well as the "Get"

Converting Carolyn's support into major sponsorship meant I had to figure out what I brought to the table. What was my currency? What did I have in my back pocket that was useful to the powerful people from whom I was asking favors? What was the quid pro quo? After much soul searching, I came up with a notional list. I had some unusual assets at my disposal. My intellectual capital, speaking skills, and global expertise were valuable and in demand. Perhaps I could offer them up to burnish the brand of a leader by volunteering, for example, to give a talk at a corporate conference or at a client event. I also commanded rare access. I couldn't conjure up Super Bowl tickets or seats on a private plane, but given my world, I could offer dinner at my home with celebrity scholars; invitations to special events at the Council on Foreign Relations, the UN, and Ivy League universities; and, most importantly, access to journalists and the media. Once I'd determined my currency, I deployed it passionately and put it to work to help potential sponsors.

Carolyn was a case in point. Although she had an enormously demanding day job (she headed up E&Y's global life sciences practice), she wanted to be more involved and better known as a champion of professional women. Her track record inside E&Y was impressive: she'd spearheaded a speaker's series for women called "Issues on Your Mind" and was a cofounder of Ernst & Young's Tri-State Women's

Professional Network. Understandably, she now wanted to increase her visibility externally and become recognized as a leading advocate for women nationwide. I was able to provide serious assistance, which ranged from helping her become a published author to ensuring she played a leadership role in my increasingly successful task force.

Looking back at that 2004–2007 period, I see that our trust-filled alliance exemplified the reciprocity between sponsor and protégé: it was a veritable embodiment of the two-way street. During the critical start-up phase, Carolyn garnered significant financial support for the task force from E&Y and others. In addition, she leveraged her connections and clout, helping me recruit female executives from companies where she had an in and I did not. In return, I made sure I came through for her. In 2004, I named her a co-chair of the task force and involved her in our first research projects. I also secured her appointment as an adjunct professor in my gender and policy program at Columbia University. These successes transformed her external brand. She became a significant voice on the national stage.

Establishing a Two-Way Street

What made this sponsorship relationship so powerful was its deep level of reciprocity and seamlessness. Initially, Carolyn sponsored me. In 2004, I urgently needed someone to bet on me, and she did. I then came through in major ways.

Indeed, for a while during the 2005–2007 period, I was the sponsor and she the protégé. Together we exemplified the transformative power of the "give" and the "get." All parties benefited: E&Y, the task force, Columbia University, Carolyn, me.

Carolyn opened the door for me at E&Y, ensuring it became a significant funder of the task force, but E&Y reaped rich rewards. The research we crafted together underpinned some important talent initiatives at E&Y and helped it brand itself as an employer of choice for women, a fact that went straight to the bottom line. The E&Y leader who took over from Carolyn, Billie Williamson, saw the firm's involvement in our work as one of its best HR investments.

Similarly, when I showcased Carolyn in the task force or sponsored her at Columbia University, I never doubted the excellence she brought to the table. Her insider knowledge of how to implement transformative change within organizations made her a natural catalyst in private-sector groups. She also proved to be a standout professor, consistently earning some of the highest ratings in my program.

Coming Through with Loyalty and Performance

In short, Carolyn and I weren't in the business of simply swapping favors. Rather, we were doing what sponsors and protégés have always done for one another. She extended my reach with her own; I built her brand by leveraging mine.

We both knew, unequivocally, that we were the real deal. We could unreservedly vouch for one another's value.

Now in its tenth year, the task force numbers some seventy-five global organizations that range from Goldman Sachs to GE to Google, and from the International Monetary Fund to the CIA. As proud as I am of our growth and the vote of confidence it represents, I'm even more gratified at the impact we've had and the action we've driven. We have moved the dial. We've empowered companies as well as individuals and moved thousands of diverse candidates up the ladder and into leadership. On the strength of our reports, books, and articles my Task Force for Talent Innovation and its associated research center, the Center for Talent Innovation, has promulgated dozens of new best practices that have changed the game, not just for women and people of color, but also for gen Y hires and members of the LGBT community. Our legacy has burnished the brands of each of us who gathered at the Century Club table that day.

In its operation as well as its origin, in its vision as well as its mission, the task force is sponsorship writ large. It positions each of our members (senior women and men in our participating companies) as advocates for a diverse group their high-potential men and women. As those individuals break through to leadership, they in turn extend their sponsorship to up-and-comers in the pipeline below. This dynamic has long seeded the C-suite with white men. With our intervention, sponsorship will now propel women and people of color into upper management. The fight for equality that began in the sixties and seventies might at long last claim victory.

A Final Note

Looking back on my journey, I'm struck by the importance of castles—and the importance of making them as magical as possible.

In 2004, as I honed my vision for CTI and the task force, I thought I'd built a pretty good castle. It certainly served me well, turbocharging my resolve as I learned to unleash the power of sponsorship.

But I perceive now that as fine a vision I'd dreamt for myself, I didn't dream big enough. I didn't know how. I didn't have role models to show me what success might truly encompass. In the wake of the extraordinary interviews I did for this book, I'm newly conscious of how widespread this problem is, especially for women. They lack, as I did, a sense of just how glorious a castle they might inhabit. The conversation around women's achievements persists in harping on the negative: the brutal sacrifices, the agonizing choices, the bitter trade-offs. That conversation has to change because success brims with rare joys and precious opportunities. These last few years have been studded with gob-smacking moments for a girl from the Welsh mining valleys: a lunch at the White House, a speech at the House of

Commons, and a Woman of the Year award. But more precious than the events and honors is the impact, agency, and influence I now have. The reason I was at that White House luncheon was to consult with the Council of Economic Advisers on a new strategy for women in President Obama's second term. I feel immensely proud as well as humbled by my newfound power.

So I say to you: Dream big. Build a magnificent castle. Adorn it, embellish it, and hold it in your mind in glorious Technicolor. It will power you through the tough times, and when you arrive, you won't be disappointed. I promise you.

Notes

Chapter 1

1. Unless otherwise cited, all quotes come from author-conducted interviews.

2. Some names and affiliations have been changed. When only first names are used, they are pseudonyms.

3. Sylvia Ann Hewlett, with Kerrie Peraino, Laura Sherbin, and Karen Sumberg, *The Sponsor Effect: Breaking Through the Last Glass Ceiling* (Boston: *Harvard Business Review* research report, December 2010).

4. Herminia Ibarra, Nancy Carter, and Christine Silva, "Why Men Still Get More Promotions Than Women," *Harvard Business Review*, September 2010, 80–85.

5. Survey data reflects the talent pipeline worldwide for the year 2007.

6. Our three-year four survey inquiry culminated in four reports:
   Sylvia Ann Hewlett et al, *The Sponsor Effect*
   Sylvia Ann Hewlett, Lauren Leader-Chivée, and Karen Sumberg with Catherine Fredman and Claire Ho, *Sponsor Effect: UK* (New York: Center for Talent Innovation, June 2012)
   Sylvia Ann Hewlett, Maggie Jackson, and Ellis Cose with Courtney Emerson, *Vaulting the Color Bar: How Sponsorship Levers Multicultural Professionals into Leadership* (New York: Center for Talent Innovation, October 2012)
   Sylvia Ann Hewlett, Melinda Marshall, and Laura Sherbin with Barbara Adachi, *Sponsor Effect 2.0: Road Maps for Sponsors and Protégés* (New York: Center for Talent Innovation, November 2012)

Chapter 2

1. Anne-Marie Slaughter, "Why Women Still Can't Have It All," *The Atlantic*, July/August 2012.

Chapter 3

1. Gail Blanke, *Throw Out Fifty Things: Clear the Clutter, Find Your Life* (New York: Grand Central Life & Style, 2010).

Chapter 5

1. See http://news.yahoo.com/struggling-bank-america-shakes-exec-ranks-225348682.html; and http://www.forbes.com/sites/halahtouryalai/2011/09/02/bank-of-americas-latest-peril-losing-merrill-lynch/.

Chapter 6

1. Nancy Carter and Christine Silva, *Mentoring Necessary But Insufficient for Advancement*, report by Catalyst Inc., December 1, 2010.

Chapter 9

1. Sheryl Sandberg, *Lean In: Women, Work, and the Will to Lead* (New York: Knopf, 2013).

2. Adrian Furnham and Tom Buchanan, "Personality, gender, and self-perceived intelligence," *Personality and Individual Differences* 39 (2005): 543–555.

3. Suzanne Doyle-Morris, *Beyond the Boys' Club: Strategies for Achieving Career Success as a Woman Working in a Male Dominated Field* (UK: Wit and Wisdom Press, 2009), 6.

4. Linda Babcock and Sara Laschever, *Women Don't Ask: The High Cost of Avoiding Negotiation—and Positive Strategies for Change* (New York: Bantam Books, 2007), 2.

5. Sylvia Ann Hewlett and Ripa Rashid, *Winning the War for Talent in Emerging Markets: Why Women Are the Solution* (Boston: Harvard Business Review Press, 2011).

Chapter 10

1. John Koblin, "Intrigue at the Times Magazine: Marzorati's Departure Followed Soured Morale and a Controversial Deputy," *New York Observer*, July 21, 2010. http://observer.com/2010/07/intrigue-at-the-times-magazine-marzoratis-departure-followed-soured-morale-and-a-controversial-deputy/2/.

2. Peter Cohan, "Was Mark Hurd Really That Good for Hewlett-Packard?" dailyfinance.com, August 8, 2010. http://www.dailyfinance.com/2010/08/08/was-mark-hurd-really-that-good-for-hewlett-packard/.

Chapter 11

1. From comments made at the launch of *The Sponsor Effect: Breaking Through the Last Glass Ceiling*, a report by the Center for Talent Innovation, New York City, January 12, 2011, published by *Harvard Business Review*, December 2010.

Chapter 12

1. Sylvia Ann Hewlett, Lauren Leader-Chivée, Laura Sherbin, and Joanne Gordon with Fabiola Dieudonné, *Executive Presence* (New York: Center for Talent Innovation, November 2012). See also Sylvia Hewlett's *Executive Presence* (New York: HarperCollins, forthcoming Spring/Summer 2014).

Index

About the Author

Sylvia Ann Hewlett is an economist and the founding president and CEO of the Center for Talent Innovation, a Manhattan-based think tank where she chairs a task force of seventy-five multinational companies focused on fully realizing the new streams of talent in the global labor market. For the last nine years she's directed the Gender and Policy Program at Columbia  University's School of International and Public Affairs. She's also co-director of the Women's Leadership Program at the Columbia Business School. She is a member of the Council on Foreign Relations and the Century Association.

Hewlett is the author of ten *Harvard Business Review* articles and ten critically acclaimed books, including *When the Bough Breaks* (winner of a Robert F. Kennedy Memorial Book Award), *Off-Ramps and On-Ramps* (named as one of the best business books of 2007 by Amazon.com), and *Winning the War for Talent in Emerging Markets*. She is currently ranked #11 on the Thinkers50 list of the world's most influential business gurus. Her writings have appeared in the *New York Times*, the *Financial Times*, *Foreign Affairs*, and the *International Herald Tribune*, and she is a featured blogger on the *HBR Blog Network*. In 2011 she received the Isabel Benham Award from the Women's Bond Club as well as a Women of the Year Award from the Financial Women's Association.

Hewlett is a founder of Hewlett Chivée Partners, an advisory services firm that focuses on helping organizations leverage talent across the divides of culture, gender, geography, and generation.

Hewlett has taught at Cambridge, Columbia, and Princeton universities and has held fellowships at the Institute for Public Policy Research in London and the Center for the Study of Values in Public Life at Harvard. In the 1980s she became the first woman to head the Economic Policy Council, a nonprofit composed of 125 business and labor leaders.

She is a frequent guest on TV and radio programs, appearing on *The Oprah Winfrey Show*, *The NewsHour with Jim Lehrer*, *Charlie Rose*, *ABC World News Tonight*, *The Today Show*, *The View*, *BBC World News*, and *Talk of the Nation*—and she has been lampooned on *Saturday Night Live*.

A Kennedy Scholar and graduate of Cambridge University, Hewlett earned her PhD in economics at London University.